Salvage Secrets

VIKING
OVEN LIGHTS
REAR
FRONT

Salvage Secrets

TRANSFORMING RECLAIMED MATERIALS INTO DESIGN CONCEPTS

Joanne Palmisano

Photographs by Susan Teare

W. W. NORTON & COMPANY · NEW YORK • LONDON

All photos are by Susan Teare, except where noted otherwise.
Illustrations by Cliff Deetjen.

Printed in Singapore
FIRST EDITION

Composition and book design by Kristina Kachele Design, llc
Manufacturing by KHL Printing Co. Pte Ltd
Production Manager: Leeann Graham
Digital Production: Joe Lops

Library of Congress Cataloging-in-Publication Data

Palmisano, Joanne.
Salvage secrets: transforming reclaimed materials into design concepts/Joanne Palmisano; photographs by Susan Teare.–1st ed.
p. cm.
Includes index.
ISBN 978-0-393-73339-6 (hardcover)
1. Salvage (Waste, etc.) in interior decoration. I. Title.

NK2115.5.S25P35 2011
747'.1—dc22
2010037268
ISBN 13: 978-0-393-73339-6

W. W. Norton & Company, Inc., 500 Fifth Avenue, New York, N.Y. 10110
www.wwnorton.com
W. W. Norton & Company Ltd., Castle House, 75/76 Wells St., London W1T 3QT
0 9 8 7 6 5 4 3 2

Contents

THE REBUILDING CENTER
TUB TOWN
TURNPIKE

Acknowledgments

I want to thank the many individuals who have given their time, support, and expertise throughout the writing of this book. First, I want to thank Susan Teare for her amazing photography, as well as her outstanding team, Lindsay Raymondjack and Toni Finnegan. Thank you to Cliff Deetjen of Peregrine Design/Build for his architectural drawings; to David Knox, owner of Mason Brothers Architectural Salvage Warehouse, for being my salvage mentor; and to Tim Frost of Peregrine Design/Build for his technical and green advice. I also want to thank interior designer and stylist extraordinaire Shannon Quimby, of the REX project, for being my best friend, having as much passion for salvage as I do, and for all her help and support of this book. A big thank you to Andrea Costella, my editor and advisor at W. W. Norton & Company, for making this book a reality and being as excited about it as I am. And to copyeditor extraordinaire, Casey Ruble, who helped me to communicate all my ideas in the best way possible. To my parents and siblings, and all my wonderful friends: Your support of all I do and your understanding my obsession for salvage means a great deal to me. Thank you! And a special thank you goes to my husband, Steve, my avid supporter, and our daughter, Gabrielle, the next-generation salvager.

There are many architects, builders, homeowners, designers, building professionals, and salvage gurus who played a key role in the making of this book. We cannot thank them enough for their interest, for opening up their businesses and homes, and for their passion for all things salvaged. Your generosity in letting me tell your story and share your passion for using salvaged goods will help us change the way we build.

In no particular order, I would also like to thank Anna and Steve Palmer; Marty Rudolph; Nicole, Max, and Sophia Gorman; Debbie and Terry Allen; Muddy Creek Stone Company; Marty Eichinger; Eichinger Sculpture Studio; Annie Fleming; Dr. Gregg and Laura Takashima; Kim Deetjen; Karin Lidbeck-Brent; Urban Spruce Interior Design; Chris Munford; Bedrock Industries; Nancy Ranchel; Sarah McCully-Posner; John Sauer; Gleenglass; Sattie Clark and Eric Kaster; Eleek; Tom Hatch; Janel Campbell at Neil Kelly; Richard and Anne De Wolf; Arciform; Ryan Walsh; DRW Design/Build; Paige Manning; Carrie Wulfman; 4 or 5 Interiors; Robert Anderson; Mike O'Brien; South Village; Jon and Jenn Pizzagalli; Randy and Shawn Sweeny; Sweeny Design/Build; Amy Gregory and Mike Worth; Glenn and Chase Hoffinger; Shane Endicott; Our United Villages; the Rebuilding Center; the ReSource Center; Mason Brothers Architectural Salvage Warehouse; Steve Conant; Conant Metal and Light; Brendan O'Reilly; Gristmill Builders; Steve Oppenheim; Steve Miller; Hippo Hardware and Trading Company; Morgan Powers; Nathan Good; Nathan Good Architects; Todd Sarandos; Jordan Wilson; Red Concrete; Chris Conner and Larry Buck; Conner & Buck; Michael Minadeo; Minadeo & Partners; Janet LaPan Babits; the ReBuild Center; Liz Shayne; Tiffany Bluemle; and Tawnya Pell. Finally, thanks to all of the homeowners who remained anonymous and all the builders, designers, and professionals who worked on these salvaged homes.

An old claw-foot tub sits in the corner of the master bathroom of this new home, inviting and calming. Other salvage design elements include the antique cabinet for bathroom supplies and the vanity, custom-made out of salvaged wood.

Author Joanne Palmisano working at her kitchen island—her favorite spot in her home. This island top was made from salvaged Douglas fir railroad trusses from an 1880s building that was torn down in a neighboring town. The vintage soapstone sink, backsplash, refrigerator, pantry door, and clock were also salvaged.

Sample piece of wood that was used in the kitchen island at left.

Introduction

I felt like Nancy Drew when I began searching for vintage salvaged wood for the kitchen island top in our home. I had some specific guidelines that I felt pretty strongly about. The wood had to be at least 2½ to 3 inches thick, the boards had to be antique with some character, and the pieces had to be long, as our island was L-shaped—11 feet and 6 feet, respectively. I began my detective work by calling a local architectural-salvage shop owner. The shop didn't have exactly what I was looking for but they gave me the number of someone who might. A farmer, also a collector of reclaimed wood, thought he had just what we were looking for. He was about an hour's drive from our

A salvaged door, with vintage knob and faceplate, provides a wonderfully welcoming feel to this bathroom, with a vintage washstand transformed into a modern bathroom vanity. When using an antique piece of furniture, such as this washstand, however, get an appraisal first. Once you alter the piece, its value plummets.

home, so my husband, our four-year-old daughter, and I went for a Sunday trip up to the farm. In the middle of a field, knee-high in snow, we uncovered a single, seemingly unremarkable piece from a haphazard pile of boards that once served as floor joists in an 1880s railroad building and brought it back to the barn. Never in a million years would I have expected anyone to look at that pile of old wood and say, "Wow, I just have to have that in my home!" But when the farmer ground away the dirt and grime with a belt sander, he revealed the true look of the wood—rich, reddish in color, fine-grained, full of character and textures. It was perfect! We took the whole pile. That was just the beginning of our fascinating search for salvaged materials that were not only unique and beautiful but affordable for our family.

DESIGNING WITH SALVAGE TODAY

Salvaged materials—that is, any material from an old building or home that is reused or repurposed in a new way—have historically suffered a bad reputation, being seen as synonymous with the words *ugly* or *expensive*. Thankfully, times, technology, and design concepts have changed, and more and more professionals and homeowners are recognizing the benefits, both aesthetic and environmental, of integrating salvaged materials into their design objectives. Modern, sleek, clean, simple, stylish, beautiful, and chic are just a few of the words now used to describe home designs that incorporate salvage materials.

Now that professionals are more willing to work with salvaged materials and companies have begun specializing in finding and selling exceptional products made out of recycled materials, designs are becoming more attractive. Both homeowners and professionals in the building trades are also embracing the very important green movement occurring across the globe, which is changing the way we live in it. We cannot ignore the fact that the building industry produces almost a third of today's waste. A study conducted by the National Association of Home Builders (NAHB) estimates that 8,000 pounds of waste is created from the construction of a 2,000-square-foot home. Much of that waste, a large majority of which is wood, can be salvaged or recycled.

With knowledge, research, and some up-front planning, today's homes can have a unique and beautiful character by incorporating materials that once

This living room addition to an 1800s farmhouse incorporates salvaged materials with modern, energy-efficient windows. The floor is made of sanded and sealed vintage barn boards, and the beams, which function not only as structural support but also as the key design feature, were also salvaged from a barn. Discarded furniture that the homeowner picked up and had reupholstered in vintage fabrics adds to the aesthetic.

would have been considered someone else's trash. In this way, we can share responsibility and respect for the places we live, as well as for how we create and live in them. Using salvaged material today will help us all tomorrow.

DEFINING THE TERMS

Many different terms exist for salvaged materials—salvaged, repurposed, recycled, reclaimed, and reused, for example. For the sake of consistency in this book, I'll stick to the word salvaged when referring to material whose basic structure has not been changed, such as a piece of wood I used for my kitchen island top. For materials whose basic structure has been changed, such as old screens that have been melted down and made into something different, like a drawer pull, I will use the term recycled. Salvaged materials can, of course, be fairly new, such as general framing wood. There are no hard-and-fast definitions for vintage or "antique," but generally vintage is used for objects over twenty years old, and antique refers to those over seventy-five years old.

Using salvaged material is more of an art than a science due to the ever-changing age, structure, size, and shape of the materials chosen—no two boards, bricks, or metal pieces are ever identical. Most of the time using salvage requires some upfront planning, especially if the material needs to be structural and has to meet building-code specifications. Many builders, designers, and architects specialize in the use of salvage and even stockpile it for future use. Inventory at salvage locations is

A new, farmhouse-style home incorporates vintage, salvaged brick to give this living room a warm, welcoming feeling. The brick was found by the builder of the home in an upstate New York salvage yard. Because not all brick is created equal—having very different looks, textures, and even structural qualities—the builder had the brick fire tested before using it for the inside firebox areas as well as the external masonry. It is important to have enough brick from the same source for your project to avoid a mishmash of colors and textures (unless, of course, that is the look you are going for).

SALVAGE LEXICON

Salvaged	The general, overarching term referring to all materials that are reused, reclaimed, or repurposed from another home, building, or other location.
Recycled	Items that are made from salvaged materials whose basic structure has been changed, such as metal scraps melted down and made into fixtures or glass pieces melted down and made into tile.
Repurposed	Items that are reused in a different area of the original home or are used in a different way, such as a patio stone reused for a staircase.
Reclaimed	Often used with wood, reclaimed materials have been brought back to life from something else, such as sunken logs made into flooring.
Reused	Often used interchangeably with recycled and reclaimed, this term basically refers to something that is the same material but used for a different purpose or location.

constantly changing and no two shops are ever the same, making it important to visit more than one on a regular basis. If you're considering products that are made with recycled materials, such as glass tiles, there is more consistency in the products.

The American Society of Interior Designers (ASID) and the U.S. Green Building Council (USGBC) have put together guidelines for green remodeling—called the REGREEN program—which touch on the use of salvaged material and give examples of homes that incorporate it. If you are looking to get LEED (Leadership in Energy and Environmental Design) points, refer to the "resource reuse" section in the MR Credit 3.

◂ This lakefront master bath incorporates salvaged pieces in a variety of ways. The countertop is made from 1880s Douglas fir that has been planed and sealed. The mirrors are made from salvaged windows and mirrors from old medicine cabinets. The tile was found in a seconds room. The door, which, left in its natural state, matched the rest of the doors in the house, was found at a salvage shop with the hardware on it.

LET'S TALK COST

Does using salvaged material cost more than buying new materials? This frequently asked question doesn't have a simple yes or no answer. Although it is true that salvaged material is often less expensive than buying brand new,

This remodeled kitchen incorporates a salvaged vintage stove, a 100-year-old sink, and an island that has a salvaged wood top and metal legs. Vintage cabinetry from a dentist's office adds to the storage space in the room without having to incorporate a built-in. These salvaged pieces complement the old wood floors as well as the modern appliances and fixtures.

the labor costs associated with installation can be higher. This isn't always the case, however—for example, installing wide planks of vintage wood flooring requires less time and money than new, narrower flooring. Other times, the cost of the salvaged piece itself may be higher, but its architectural significance will add overall value to the home. Likewise, a salvaged piece can sometimes add so much character to a room that a more modest, less expensive design is all that's needed. A salvaged countertop, for example, which can range from affordable to expensive, can be the masterpiece of a kitchen, allowing the surrounding cabinetry to be kept simple and low-cost.

Careful planning is another important part of the cost. Say, for example, that your builder has put in the door jambs and you show up with antique salvaged doors. Guess what? He is going to have to pull out those jambs and rebuild them to fit the older doors. Likewise, a vintage sink may not fit perfectly in the hole the builder has left for a double-bowl sink. The earlier you tell the builders about the salvaged materials you plan to use, the more responsive they will be to using them and the less additional cost you will incur.

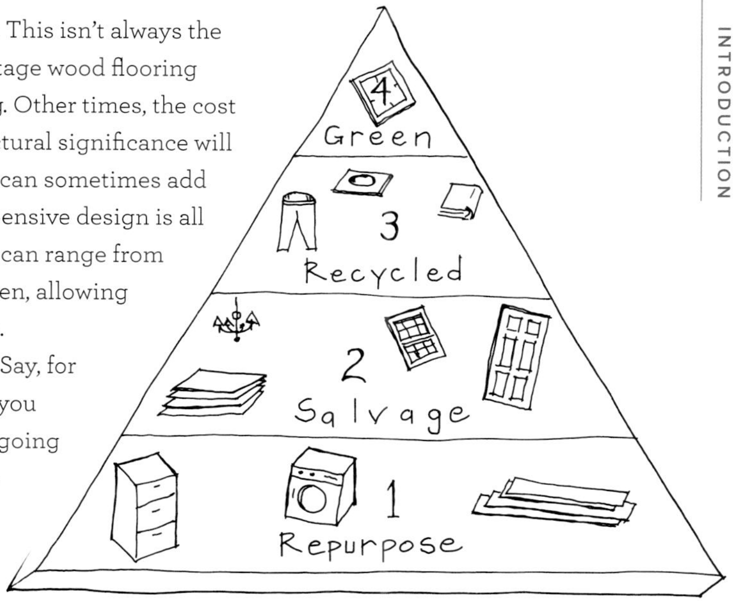

The Salvaged Materials Pyramid can help you decide how and when to incorporate salvaged material into your home's design. Whether you are building new, remodeling, or adding on, consider the pyramid and the best way to use salvaged material. Illustration by Cliff Deetjen.

THE SALVAGED MATERIALS PYRAMID

As the USDA's food pyramid shows, there are some foods we should get more of because we know they are good for our body. The same can be said of salvaged materials, which keep our planet healthy and, in turn, allow us to stay healthy as well. The bottom tier indicates what we should be using the most of when we design with salvaged materials—it represents the most sustainable way to use salvaged material.

Tier #1. Repurposed

Rather than buying a salvaged material, consider repurposing something you already have—that is, take an item already in your home and change or move it to look different or to serve a different purpose. The dark wood cabinets can be sanded and painted white (with low-VOC paint), or moved to the basement laundry or craft area. Or give or sell them to someone else—a friend, a salvage

This laundry room is a great example of repurposing. During a home-renovation project, the homeowners moved their kitchen cabinets, countertop, and sink into their laundry room, creating a very functional space.

center, an Ebay buyer, or a recycle center. There are numerous ways to salvage almost everything you want to change out. Appliances, fixtures, wood, cabinets, hardware, metal, glass, windows, concrete, tile, stone, and even insulation can be salvaged and repurposed. The little bit of effort it takes is worth keeping all these materials out of our already-overburdened landfills. We have got to be part of the change. And it starts here: Repurpose it!

Tier #2. Salvaged

When you are ready to build or renovate, salvaged materials can be used for any number of items you may need. Flooring, doors, metals, appliances, fixtures, hardware, glass, tiles—all of these things can be found at local or regional salvage shops, recycle centers, or even online from someone in your area. When you know what salvaged materials you are going to use in advance, you can create a design whose character comes from the materials themselves. Reuse, reuse, reuse: That is the mantra you should use when creating design concepts. Of course, local salvage is best, but if you need to broaden your range, all it takes is a bit of searching online. The Resources section at the end of this book will help find the perfect salvaged item for your home.

Tier #3. Recycled

This category refers to salvaged materials that have been recreated into something entirely new—for example, denim jeans turned into insulation, or newspaper into countertops, Glass from bottles,

This salvaged 1800s soapstone laundry sink was purchased at a stone company that sold both salvage and new products. Backsplash pieces were found in a scrap pile at the same shop. The cabinetry and design of the kitchen was kept simple, allowing the salvaged pieces to stand out.

Tiles recycled from salvaged glass are a focal point in the kitchen backsplash of this modern, energy-efficient home. Their rich, warm, brick color give the kitchen a sense of style, depth, and character.

windows, and doors can be recycled into windowsills, tiles, countertops, or lighting fixtures; aluminum cans can become sinks, tile, and plank flooring; and objects made of brass, copper, or steel, can be turned into drawer pulls, switch plates, light fixtures, and countertops. The list is endless.

Although there are environmental costs in transforming the material, some small, some larger, the benefit of using recycled materials is that you can have more standardization on custom pieces made and in a quantity that works for your design project. When looking for recycled products, be aware that some cannot be 100% percent recycled. For example, a nonrecycled adhesive or aggregate may be needed to bind the product together, or nonrecycled elements may be needed for structural or aesthetic purposes. In these cases, strive to find products that have 75% or more salvaged material in them. Every little bit helps.

This contemporary concrete sink, made with salvaged glass that was crushed into a powder aggregate and then added to the concrete mix, shows that products made from salvaged material do not need to be rustic, old, or dirty. They can be whatever you want them to be.

GET THE FACTS

Not all recycled materials are created equal. Green, recycled, eco-friendly, these are words that are thrown around a lot. When you choose to use a product or even a process in building or remodeling a home, it is important to get the facts. Is a product advertised as "green" actually just 5% recycled content and 95% toxic glue? Or is it 75% recycled or even better, with natural adhesives, binders, and aggregates? Once you know the facts you can make better decisions—and, if necessary, compromises.

▸ This unique master bathroom was designed around salvaged pieces. The large marble pieces came from a New Hampshire college dormitory and the sinks (with fixtures), from a Rhode Island hotel. These pieces and the antique mirror, wall sconces, and Victorian-period tiles were all found in salvage and antique shops.

Tier #4. Green

The word green is being used more and more frequently, but what does it really mean? Basically, it refers to products that are the best choices for our environment and are as local as possible. Do a little research. Does the product have to travel far? Does it take a lot of energy to create? Does it upset endangered habitats? Does it use toxic chemicals that could cause off-gassing? When using repurposed, salvaged, or recycled materials isn't an option, try to use materials that are as green as possible. Choosing eco-friendly, long-lasting materials and using quality building practices will lead us all down a road to better buildings and a healthier planet.

ABOUT THIS BOOK

There are hundreds, even thousands, of items that can be salvaged and reused in home design projects. This book touches on some of the main materials that are usually in abundance in salvage and recycle centers: wood, glass, metal, stone, and lighting. But you don't have to stop there—there are many salvaged items, one-of-a-kind or common—that can be reused in building design. For example, recycled plastic is used in many home products as well as newspaper and even old clothing.

Each chapter is dedicated to a different material. They begin by presenting the materials themselves and go on to discuss ways and locations in the home in which you can use them, as well as the structural, functional, and aesthetic

issues you should consider. Dealing with installation and finishes is touched on, along with a few of the challenges you may come across.

Because every salvaged material is different—and the ways to use them, endless—this book is not written as a "how-to" but rather as a way to offer general design concepts for inspiration. Professional architects, contractors, or salvage specialists should, of course, be consulted for expert guidance on all technical matters. There are no standard practices when it comes to using unique, reclaimed, salvaged, vintage, or recycled materials. That is part of what makes working with these materials so exciting—as well as what makes it challenging. My hope is that this not only will help you identify the structural and functional issues that need to be researched, but also inspire you to begin your own rewarding salvage journey.

◂ Built to replicate an old farmhouse, this new home incorporates numerous salvaged materials, including old wood used to create doors and frames. The stone steps were repurposed from the property while creating the landscaping. The end result is a welcoming entranceway that feels like it has been there for hundreds of years.

▸ Author arranging tiles at a recycling center.

A show-stopping stairwell and dining area in this home display a variety of ways salvaged wood can be used while paying homage to nature. The stair treads are salvaged Douglas fir planed and sanded to soften the edges. The tree trunk around which the banister curves was in a nearby barn for years; the homeowners stripped off the bark and left the trunk in its original form. The Y-shaped supporting pieces are from a salvaged section of cottonwood that the builder had stored in his barn. The stones were also salvaged, some from the property itself and other pieces from a friend's home after a landscaping project. The custom-made dining-room light was made from a spruce branch in the backyard of the property. The trim and beams were salvaged from the same wood, but planed and sanded. The table was a "first cut" (live edge), which was in a discard pile before the homeowners had it pulled out and made into a one-of-a-kind dining-room table.

Wood

When you walk into a room filled with salvaged wood, do you find yourself at peace? The warm character of the old wood evokes feelings of strength, endurance, connectedness to the natural world, and a sense of times long since past. It invites us in and welcomes us home.

Reclaimed, antique, vintage—these are some of the terms that can be applied to salvaged wood. Although these terms describe different types of wood and their specific ages, such as antique heart of pine, salvaged refers to wood that has already been used and is ready to be put to use again.

When homeowners, builders, or designers think of salvaged wood, they may picture a rustic style—a country home with dark floors and lots of knots in the wood. But this is just one of many beautiful options. Modern, classic, simple, clean, pickled, rustic, paneled, stained, glossy, rough—whatever the idea, design, or style, it can all start with salvaged wood.

Some have a natural affinity toward salvaged wood and appreciate its beauty and functionality. Others may wonder why they should even consider using salvaged wood when freshly cut wood is so readily available. There are many reasons.

First, much of today's harvested wood comes from sustainable and managed forests, but not all is. Many kinds of wood, including exotic species, grow in endangered rain forests where trees are being rapidly depleted. The harvesting of this wood results in loss of animal habitats and

DESIGN TIP

Old-growth wood is superior to farmed wood because there are more growth rings per square inch, which means higher quality. It is like thread count—the more rings, the stronger the material. An older piece of wood has a finer grain and a richer color (due to oxidation) than new wood. A finer grain is a sign of an old-growth tree from a natural forest where trees grow slowly in the shade of one another, unlike trees grown on tree farms. The tighter the growth circles in the wood, the harder the wood will be. In some cases, a piece of salvaged old-growth wood can be as hard as a steel beam!

watersheds as well as worsened air quality, not to mention the detrimental impact it has on the very people who live in these areas. If you do choose to use new wood in your building project, choose carefully. Look for local or certified wood. (Certified wood usually has a Forest Stewardship Council—FSC—label on it or is labeled by another recognized organization that determines if the wood comes from managed, sustainable lands.) Wood is a renewable resource that we are lucky to have an abundance of, but, like all natural resources, it should never be taken for granted. A study conducted by the Food and Agriculture Organization of the United Nations (FAO) showed that worldwide, we have slowed our deforestation rate from that in the 1990s. But even with tree-planting programs in many countries around the world, FAO cited a net loss of forests from 2000–2010 equivalent to the size of Costa Rica (12.84 million acres). It is time to seriously consider using reclaimed wood in all home-building and design projects, especially when considering exotic wood from countries that are deforesting at an alarming rate.

The second reason to consider using older reclaimed wood is that age lends a very special color and character to it. As wood ages, it begins to look different, and the difference is not just noticeable among different types of trees, such as cherry versus oak or beech versus fir, but even within a species itself. For example, vintage pumpkin pine is an eastern white pine that has been aged in a specific way to have a pumpkin color throughout the piece of wood. Salvaged wood tells a story through its grain, insect holes, nail marks, and other various

◂ This doorway is a perfect example of how to let the salvaged material speak for itself in the design. These massive salvaged beams, planed and cut at an angle, make for a dramatic entryway to a bedroom and the backyard.

This mountainside retreat used salvaged old-growth Douglas fir, an exceptionally strong wood. The 2 x 12 planks were listed for sale in the newspaper by a person who had them stored for 80 years in his barn. The homeowner split them and tongue and grooved them into 1 x 11 pieces to accommodate the square footage of the home. They were oiled and left to weather naturally.

textures and colors. Although many try to replicate the look of vintage wood by banging up a piece of new wood and using stain finishes to copy, nothing can replace the look and feel that Mother Nature and time can create. Design details and character can be expensive to achieve if you choose size over substance, but salvaged wood is an easy solution that adds an immense amount of personality to any building project without requiring a lot of extra work.

The third reason to consider using salvaged wood is that it has already been harvested and is ready to be used in another home project. Selecting it is an earth-friendly way to reuse building materials and avoid the energy expenditure necessary to manufacture from raw materials. Using these kinds of salvaged products is an easy way to start the green building process.

When considering salvaged wood for a project, pay attention to where it comes from as well as the overall design style and the structural integrity (discussed later in this chapter). Although using salvaged wood—or any salvaged material for that matter—is an environmentally friendly decision, it can be counterproductive if the wood is taken from a faraway location that requires lengthy transport and energy expenditure. Salvaged wood is one of the most accessible building materials and is almost always readily available locally. If the entire industry reused more leftover building materials and waste from demolition projects, we would have more products to choose from, not to mention less to dispose of.

The stairway railings of this vacation home were made from 6 x 6 salvaged old-growth Douglas fir from an apple warehouse. The wood was originally painted white, the homeowner planed and sanded them and coated them with clear Waco oil. The handmade Tiffany-like light fixture, once used as a floor lamp, was brought from another home and repurposed into a ceiling pendant.

TYPES OF SALVAGED WOOD

Numerous species of reclaimed wood are readily available today. Most reclaimed wood comes from deconstruction sites such as barns, mills, wooden dams, warehouses,

Older pieces of wood, such as old-growth Douglas fir and wide planks of pine, are usually found in architectural salvage shops or specialty wood locations. These pieces of wood, left in their natural state, with a clear finish or sealer, are great for floors or use in other locations where the natural character, color, and richness of the wood is allowed to shine through.

factories, vintage homes, and, of course, from construction sites. Some comes from the bottom of lakes where logs may have sunk a hundred years ago, and some comes from urban settings where trees are removed because they have become a hazard, are dying, or are growing in a lot slated for new construction. Many native woods, such as cypress, oak, ash, fir, hickory, spruce, chestnut, butternut, and cherry were often used to build barns and outbuildings because they were readily available at the time the structures were built. Over time these slow-growing woods have become less available and more expensive.

Recovering this wood when buildings are torn down is a cost-effective alternative. Learn a little about the wood you like—its colors, and the finishes that work best with it. Sometimes it takes a bit of detective work to find what you are looking for, but the time and effort is worth it.

The rich color of the salvaged wood in this contemporary home blends beautifully with the more modern kitchen and stone floor.

‣ This master-bedroom wall is a perfect example of working the design around the salvage pieces rather than setting on a design and then finding the material. As an architect, the homeowner used his knowledge and the leftover materials from a variety of projects on which he was working to create a wall of salvaged pieces of wood—plywood, trim, cedar shingles. The artful end result, which looks like a jigsaw puzzle, hides a large closet and the door to the master bathroom.

Softwood Versus Hardwood

Hardwood trees, like maple, birch, beech, oak, and fruit trees, have broad leaves and are deciduous. Softwood trees, such as fir, pine, spruce, and hemlock, are conifers (also called evergreens), which means they do not flower and use cones to reproduce.

The type of wood is usually a less important consideration than its size, color, and intended use. For example, softwoods are more readily available in wide planks, so they might be a better choice if you're making an island or countertop. A hardwood might be a good choice for flooring because it can better withstand wear and tear than softwoods. If you're looking for wood to use as wall paneling or wainscoting, softwood left in its original state or sealed in a matte finish can have an exceptional patina and character, and wear won't be an issue if the wood is used on the wall.

Dimensional Lumber (Basic Reclaimed Framing-Type Wood)

When thinking of salvaged wood, most people picture vintage wood, but dimensional lumber (two-by-fours, two-by-sixes, etc.) reclaimed from a recent demolition project or leftover from a current building project also counts as salvaged even though it is relatively new. "Vintage" salvaged wood is considered by many in the wood and salvage field to be over fifty years old; the term "antique" salvaged wood is usually reserved for wood that is closer to a hundred years old or more. What we call "basic" salvaged dimensional lumber, which can be found at recycle centers, does not have that older weathered look or the color or character that older wood has. But various stains and finishes can be used to transform these pieces into something special.

The color, width, relative hardness, and style of the wood are the most important variables to consider when selecting wood for a project. Exposure to weather, age, oxidation, insect or worm holes, and human wear and tear all add character to wood, and the older it is and the more exposure it gets, the more character the wood usually portrays. For example, if you are designing a home around an amazing open floor plan, the look and feel of the floors will play a huge role in the aesthetics of the space. This is where vintage or antique wood would be a huge advantage. But if you are designing a beach cottage and want

to paint, stain, or whitewash wood for paneled walls, basic salvaged dimensional lumber could be used, as the natural look of the wood wouldn't be as important.

POSSIBLE USES

Highly versatile, wood can be used in almost any location in a home. Whether you're using it for structural elements such as posts and beams or for cosmetic features such as trim, wood provides a feeling of warmth and comfort.

Author Joanne Palmisano inspects a piece of dimensional lumber. Most of today's lumber is kiln-dried, which forces the water out of the wood. This can sometimes cause a piece of wood to warp. Palmisano is also inspecting it for nail holes, splits, and other issues that will help her decide how it can be used.

The same piece of dimensional lumber was cut into six pieces to show the different looks that can be achieved with just a little bit of paint or stain. The upper left is an ebony stain, the upper middle is a redwood stain, the upper right was painted a glossy black, the lower left was whitewashed, the lower middle was painted blue and then sanded for a cottage look, and the last piece is a glossy white. There are thousands of ways to use paints, stains, and finishes on salvaged dimensional wood to create a specific look and style.

A wonderful example of a painted wood floor and cabinetry. A vintage schoolhouse light fixture adds to the design.

Plywood, one of the most common salvaged materials at recycle and rebuild centers, is rarely thought of for home design. Yet it can be cut into a variety of shapes and sizes and used as flooring, wall covering, stairs, cabinetry, and more. These dimensions were used by a sculptor who was converting a warehouse into a studio and apartment. With only two cuts, he was able to create three pieces that could be fit together at a variety of angles for the floor in his live-work space.

These plywood pieces were laid in various patterns and glued down (each piece was weighted while the glue dried). They were then stained, grouted, and covered with a few coats of sealer. A conversation piece in itself, this floor was the perfect affordable, aesthetically pleasing solution for a large space that gets a lot of traffic.

Floors

Floors are the most common use for salvaged wood. As a large component of the interior design, they act as a canvas for the rest of the project. Wood floors left in their natural state (with a clear finish) add warmth to a home and allow a blank slate for any style. Painted floors can dramatically change the look of a home—whitewashed floors work well in a beach cottage; floors painted a solid glossy white, gray, or other color can pop in a modern loft; a painted checkerboard pattern can bring a sense of history or even fun to a historic farmhouse or electic-style house. Salvaged wood floorboards or pieces of wood (including plywood) are extremely versatile and can be adapted, with a stain, whitewash, or other unique finish to meet every need and style.

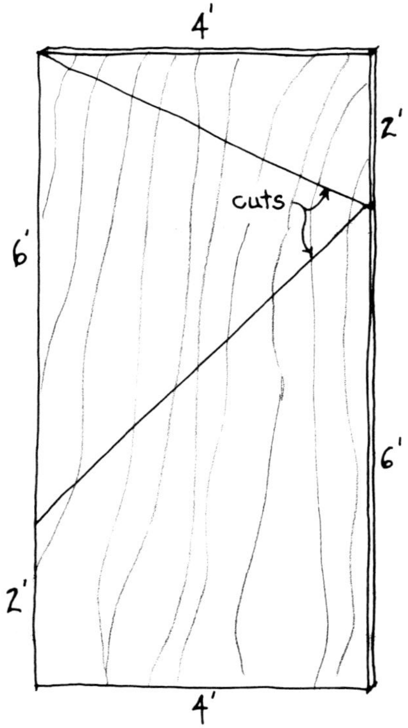

This view shows many of the unique, affordable ways the sculptor/homeowner used salvaged materials. The high concrete countertop was repurposed in its full length from his old studio, which was being transformed into loft apartments. He also repurposed the old doors from his studio, which he originally purchased at an architectural salvage shop. The baker's table is from a bakery that went out of business and was selling its equipment—a fine example of using an interesting, functional piece that is much more affordable than built-in cabinetry. The round structural pole was salvaged from the bottom of a nearby river, and the alder tree at the corner of the cabinetry (far right) had fallen a few years earlier and was lying in a friend's yard. The flooring is salvaged plywood pieces.

The wood in this living room is repurposed barn board. The brick on the fireplace was also salvaged, as well as the stair railing, which once served as a beam in the home. The flooring is salvaged pine. Together, these salvaged pieces create a design that feels cozy and intimate.

Walls

Vertical or horizontal planks, bead board, and old v-groove wall panels are popular on walls. Using salvaged wood for half-wall wainscoting with a top trim piece or a full wall (and ceiling) of horizontal planking, whitewashed or painted a high-gloss white, lends a level of detail, character, and depth to a room that is rarely seen in today's homes. These details add a tremendous "wow factor" to a space and can be easily accommodated in the plans.

This bathroom counter makes use of the tree's natural form with a living edge. The salvaged wood and simple style of the bathroom show how natural materials can work well with modern details.

Counters

Using salvaged wood for counter space is one of the most affordable design solutions—and also one of the most misunderstood. Many homeowners are nervous about using wood in a space that sees a lot of water, gets heavy use, and contains food products. But with the proper, nontoxic sealers, wood will weather well in a kitchen and bathroom. Of course it is helpful if water is not left to sit on the counters and wiped off to keep the finish working its best. If

water does get under the sealer, a little sanding and resealing is recommended. Many older kitchens, such as those from the 1910s and 1920s, used butcher block from old-growth maple or birch. These salvaged butcher-block counters look amazing (and almost brand new) after using a belt sander to clean up the top ⅛ inch. When using soft woods as counters, whether in the kitchen, bathroom, or office, it is important to know that it can dent easily; a runner or decorative tablecloth is an effective remedy. No matter what type of counter material is chosen (wood, metal, glass, etc.) an untreated butcher block or trivet is always recommended for cutting or placement of any extremely hot or cold item.

Cabinets

Salvaged cabinetry works in one of two ways. You can reuse already-existing cabinets or create cabinetry out of recycled or repurposed wood. Reused cabinets can vary in quality; some are solid wood and others may be pressed particle board. Some may be tongue and groove whereas others are held together by brackets. The cabinetry chosen should be

◂ Cabinetry is one of the most expensive elements of a kitchen. Repurposed cabinetry (painted or outfitted with new hardware) is the best option but when that isn't possible, salvaged wood can be used to make new cabinetry. When looking at cabinetry for repurposing, check for structural soundness. These homeowners removed their cabinetry during a renovation project, sanded it down, and repainted it a welcoming red color. They dramatically changed the look of their kitchen without spending a lot of money.

▸ Wood furnishings can be used as an alternative to built-in cabinetry—old bureaus and vintage dressers as vanities, pine cupboards as pantries, armoires as closets. The owner of this home—which mixes Arts and Crafts and Asian styles—used a vintage dresser as a guest-bathroom vanity. She placed a piece of glass on the top and used a stone bowl she already owned as the sink. This allowed the unique character of top of the antique piece to show through; a regular countertop made of stone or other type of material would have hidden the details of the piece. The flooring in the hall was repurposed oak from another room, stained a dark walnut brown to give a rich color.

structurally sound and all hardware tightened to ensure a solid fit. With a little sanding, paint, and hardware, reused cabinetry can be given an entirely new look. And don't forget about unique vintage or antique furniture pieces that can be repurposed as cabinetry in the kitchen and bathroom. Creating cabinetry from salvaged wood allows for more variety in style, as you have the flexibility to specify the layout and design you want. Any type of wood can be used for cabinetry; even recycled doors can be cut in half to make cabinet doors. Wainscoting can also be used to create a paneled-cabinetry look.

Mantels and Fireplace Surrounds

We have all seen intricately detailed vintage fireplace surrounds or stone fireplaces with massive vintage beams as mantels; these elements draw us into a room and stand out as focal points. But the design surrounding a fireplace or wood or gas stove can be as simple as one linear piece of salvaged material across the top or several pieces surrounding the firebox (or gas stove or insert) on all three sides. Wood around a fireplace always needs to be placed well away

from the heat by inserting a transitional piece, usually made of stone, brick, or tile, between the direct heat and the decorative part of the fireplace. An architect, contractor, or mason will be able to advise you on proper methods and techniques to conform to fire-safety codes, as well as ensure proper draft and aesthetic.

Trim

Window or interior salvaged trim millwork can be found in natural colors, but most trim has paint on it. Some of it may be chipped; some of it may have layer upon layer so that the paint gives the piece another stylistic element.

Some older trim pieces have exceptional detail; others are straight, with no rounded or detailed edges. These pieces, usually 3 to 5 inches in width, can be cut to create a variety of items—the frame for an interior window, cabinet facing, ceiling wainscoting, or crown molding. If the linear footage is sufficient,

▲ Salvaged trim can be found in most rebuild centers. Use it as is or create new pieces from it, such as cabinetry, doors, ceiling or wall bead board, or even fireplace surrounds.

◀ This fireplace shows that new can be created from old. The salvaged brick, vintage metalwork, and trim pieces that create the mantel and surround work well together around a new energy-efficient gas-fireplace insert.

it can be used as trim throughout the house.

Doors

Wooden interior doors can be found in abundance, but finding several identical ones can be a bit more challenging. There are standard sizes for interior doors (most common is about 30 inches or 2'6," as it is commonly called) but older vintage doors from the 1880s or early 1900s can range from 24 to 30 inches. Knowing the size ahead of time allows you to integrate doors into the design project without any surprises. Vintage wood doors add a tremendous amount of character to rooms. The craftsmanship and detail in the wood on many older doors is hard to find in newer doors. Hallways lined with natural-colored vintage wood doors or an entranceway door that is built from solid mahogany can give quite a punch to the design. Old barn doors or doors with stained-glass panels or pebbled glass are fabulous on runners in front of a pantry or used as semi-privacy doors to a sunroom or office. Smaller vintage doors can be used for hallway, bathroom, or bedroom closets, when space for a swing door or large closet is an issue. Another option, of course, is to build your own custom doors from salvaged wood.

▶ Using salvaged wood and a few vintage metal pieces, this family created a half door that allows a view into the mudroom without letting the dogs have free roam of the house. The antique barrels hold the family's favorite sports tools and take care of the family's recycling needs. This kind of half door can be made from salvaged wood or created by cutting a salvaged door in half.

◀ The master-bathroom cabinetry here was created from trim salvaged from the home that was torn down on the same property. The original paint was left on the pieces. These unique cabinet doors complement the more modern concrete counter with recycled glass aggregate, the new drop-in sinks, and the fixtures. Along with the salvaged flooring, the vintage mirror, sign, and wall sconces add up to amazing style in this bathroom, showing that salvaged materials can be used to create one-of-a-kind designs.

Posts and Beams

Ceiling beams, structural posts, mantels—salvaged post-and-beams can be used in a variety of ways. They can visually separate a space without being an integral part of the structure, like a wall. Or they can be structural and exposed, serving as the design itself. A vintage or reclaimed post at the end of a stairwell, sometimes an otherwise forgotten piece of design can offer significant style and a sense of place in the space. The style of the home will determine the type of salvaged post chosen. Posts can also be added as a structural element to a kitchen island, a unique touch that gives the island a cozier look.

STRUCTURAL ELEMENTS TO CONSIDER

When using salvaged wood, choose wisely and research the sources. For example, some salvaged wood—such as a thin pine floor from an older home or barn wall siding—can be full of splits and will not hold up well to pressure or a lot of use, making it better suited wall coverings or other stylistic elements. Rot or extensive insect damage are two common flaws to watch out for. Many vintage woods have worm or insect holes that add a tremendous amount of

The old beams throughout this home play a key structural role in the open floor plan but function aesthetically as well. Left in their natural state, they are the perfect backdrop for this kitchen cocktail sink.

◀ A salvaged bathroom door placed on an overhead slider, a salvaged bedroom door with high windows, and a salvaged entranceway closet door with a French diamond-paned glass window are a win-win-win. These three doors are just a few examples of the options available and the many locations where doors can be used as key design elements in your home. The floors in this awe-inspiring home were made from recycled pickle barrels.

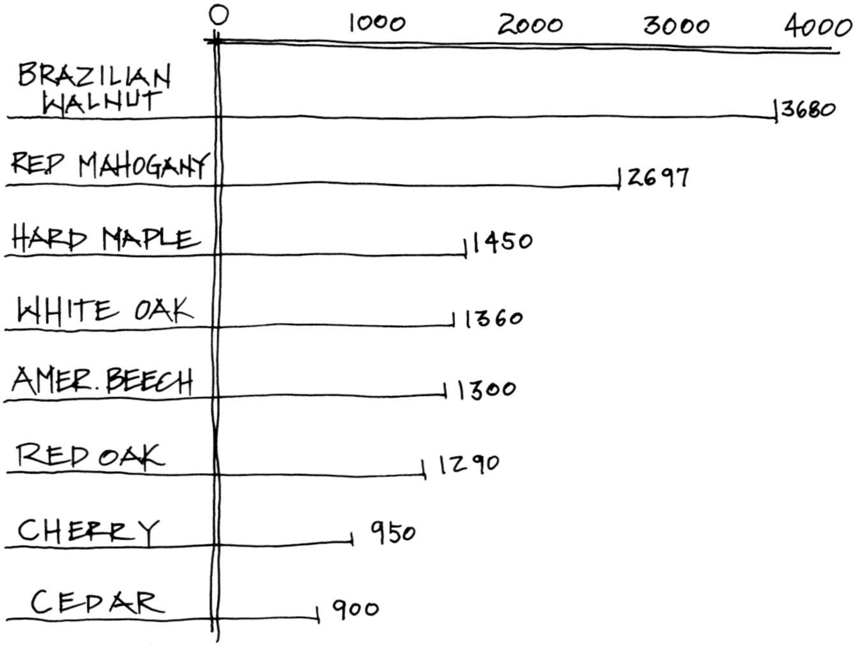

character to the wood; termite damage, on the other hand, severely affects the integrity of the wood, causing it to crumble like a graham cracker. A salvaged wood company, an architectural salvage professional, or an expert at a recycling facility should be consulted to determine the best wood for the project. That professional will go through the inventory and help select the best, straightest, and most structurally sound wood for your specific needs.

When determining the hardness of a piece of wood—that is, the structural rigidity, or pounds of force per square inch it can withstand—many professionals use the Janka Hardness Scale as a standard. The Janka chart, which can be found on the Internet, can help you determine which wood product is best for specific projects and uses, especially if the material is going to be used in a structural way.

Remember that the hardness of a wood is not necessarily determined by its classification as a hardwood or softwood. Old-growth softwood, for example,

▲ This chart shows a few pieces of the woods listed in the the Janka Hardness Scale, which can be used as a guideline when you are unsure of the hardness of the salvaged wood you are considering.

◀ The newel post in the foreground of this picture deserves a standing ovation. The white stairs and railing and the simple treads allow the vintage post to take center stage.

◂ This post-and-beam home is stunning. Floors salvaged from typewriter-factory timbers make it that much more interesting.

▸ A perfect view of the growth rings of wood. This end-cut floor in a dramatic lakefront home was made from 1800s timber from a decommissioned dam. The pieces of wood show how tight the growth rings are on trees grown in a natural forest. The tighter the rings, the harder the wood. This is one of the many reasons salvaged old-growth wood is so revered.

KNOW WHAT YOU NEED

What are you using the salvaged wood for? Know what you need before beginning your hunt for it.

Size Does the length and width match what you need? Many salvaged woods will need to lose a few inches at the ends, so bear that in mind when measuring.

Color Sand a small piece to reveal the underlying color of the wood.

Structural Integrity Look for splits, warping, and rot. Old worm holes or nail holes can give wood character without affecting it structurally, unless there is serious insect infestation.

Type Is it a softwood or hardwood? Softwoods tend to scratch and dent more easily but can have a beautiful patina when finished.

can be very hard due to the number of growth rings, and a young hardwood grown on a tree farm can be relatively soft due to the fact that it has grown quickly with a lot of space and sun.

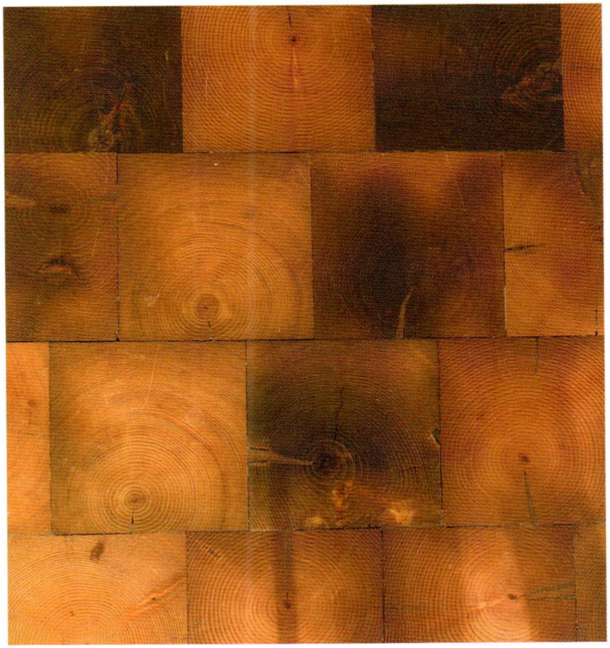

The Stability, Size, and Width of Reclaimed Wood

A piece of wood can undergo permutations over time depending on where and how it's being used, so it's important to think about its placement when determining the best size, shape, and style.

FLOORS Wood used as flooring needs to be a certain thickness—generally about three-quarters of an inch after it has been planed—so choose salvaged wood that has enough thickness to allow for that. If the wood has already been planed or will be sanded only slightly, the original ¾-inch thickness will be sufficient. Other issues to consider when thinking about floors: movement, shrinking or expanding, buckling, crowning (center bowing), or cupping (edges lifting up). The quality of wood, the density of grain, the drying of the boards, and the cut of the

▾ Salvaged beams wait for owners at a architectural salvage shop. The beams can be split and made into counters, used as exposed beams in a home for aesthetic effect or even used as structural beams in the house. They can be left in their natural state, a grayish color, or sanded (and planed) to bring out the color of the wood underneath.

▸ The beams and wall caps here were salvaged, and the bench, table, shelving, chestnut wall panels, and metal candelabras were repurposed from the original home during the remodeling project, giving this new addition an old-world flair.

grain all play a role in the stability of each board, so it's important to buy from a reputable professional who is knowledgeable and can offer site-specific advice. Other types of salvaged wood besides vintage or antique boards can also be used for flooring—salvaged plywood or pressed board, for example, or salvaged dimensional lumber or even the end cuts of beams.

BEAMS Vintage beams used for structural purposes must be the right thickness and dimension to support the weight they have to hold. Weak, rotting beams should never be used for structural purposes, even when they are the right dimensions.

Cake

◀ Here the owner received a salvaged beam from an old home that was being renovated and cut it to make a wonderfully thick countertop for an in-law apartment tucked away in her newly constructed barn. The character, thickness, and color of this countertop enhance this tiny kitchen. The salvaged vintage pendant hanging over the sink adds a sense of warmth and fun. The concrete floor, a greenish color, was made with salvaged aggregate.

▶ The shelves of this library room built with new wood, are topped with a beautiful salvaged piece purchased from a local farmer. Sanded slightly, the countertop wood was left in its natural form and then sealed. The thickness of the salvaged piece gives the bookshelves substance as well as a sense of depth. The natural color of wood against the white cabinetry and books is also an effective contrast.

DESIGN TIP

When cutting salvaged wood for countertops, islands, cabinets, mantels, stair treads, and railings, it is important to blend in the cut edge so it doesn't look different from the rest of the piece. Ways to do that include staining or even rubbing ashes from the fireplace on it and banging the end and edges of the wood with a variety of objects to dent it a bit before putting on the finish.

COUNTERTOPS AND MANTELS

When selecting wood for countertops and mantles, choose pieces that are especially thick. Thin pieces of wood will look weak and out of balance on surfaces with large bases or heavy stonework. Counter- and island tops should be about 1½ to 3 inches thick, and mantel size should be determined on a case-by-case basis—many will need the thickness of a salvaged beam rather than an individual piece of wood. All the other structural considerations mentioned apply as well.

CHALLENGES WITH SALVAGED WOOD

A common misconception about reclaimed wood is that it requires more maintenance than new wood, but that is rarely the case. The difference in "maintenance" is related only to the type of wood and finishes used. Moisture content is a consideration when working with any kind of wood. A piece of wood expands and contracts with the moisture level in the home and in the wood. When the moisture levels are low, as often happens during the drier months of winter, the floorboards will shrink, leaving gaps between the planks. When moisture levels are high, as in summer, the floorboards will expand. The expansion and contraction of wood is a natural occurrence that has to be accounted for whether it is used for flooring, wall paneling, or as a structural element. Care should be taken to store wood in conditions that approximate those inside the home.

Air-dried wood (dried naturally and evenly over time) is better than kiln-dried wood, in which the water was forced out of it. Air-dried wood has fewer warping issues than kiln-dried. Ask how your wood was dried and look at the wood carefully for warping issues.

Uncovering the Character

Unless the wood is basic framing or flooring material pulled out of a recent building, you won't see the true character of older salvaged wood until you get past the outer layer. Reclaimed wood from older houses, buildings, and barns will look old, dirty, and dusty until it is slightly sanded or planed, making it challenging to visualize the way it will look in your home. Sometimes you have to have a bit of faith in the wood and a gut instinct that it will work for your project.

Time

Architectural salvage and recycle shops rarely have ready-to-install wood like you find in big box stores, where you can grab it new off the shelf and it's ready to go. Usually salvaged wood needs to be sanded down, planed, and cut to fit the

◀ Thanks to all the salvaged materials used, it is hard to believe this is a new home. The mantel in the living room is a beam that was found in a New Hampshire salvage shop. The paneling is from an old home that was deconstructed; both it and the vintage metal grate were purchased at a local architectural shop. The flooring is from a 1790s home; the planks, some of which are up to 23 inches wide, were planed, sanded, and sealed. The stone was recovered from the property. Together, these pieces give the room the look of an authentic 1800s home.

▼ This illustration of a staircase shows how creative you can get in a salvage design. Mismatch some salvaged banister rails onto a thick beam rail, crisscrossing them so they meet code, and end the staircase with an interesting newel post. The stair treads can be as simple as painted salvaged dimensional lumber.

▸ The pine ceiling and wall paneling in this new lakefront home were repurposed from the family's old cottage, which was torn down on the same property.

project's specifications. But the extra work will pay off, because the floor, walls, cabinetry, or whatever it is you're creating will look unlike anything you could get off the shelf, and your home design will shine, raising its value.

Cost

The cost of salvaged wood varies greatly—if you get it from the farmer down the street, it may be dirt cheap; if you buy planed and finished antique wood from a company that specializes in antique lumber, it will cost more. The type and age of salvaged wood, the prep work, and the labor involved to install it will all play a role in the overall cost. Old wood doors will cost about the same or less than a new basic wood door, but the cost of installation may be higher if the doors do not come with the frames and need to be adjusted to fit the new doorways. When weighing all the pros and cons of using salvaged wood, it is important to know your priorities: your budget, the look and feel of the home you want to achieve, and its character. All of these aspects will help in your decision-making process.

Lead Issues

Some of the paint you find on older wood may be lead-based, so it is important to take precautions when cutting and sealing the wood. If you are unsure whether the paint is lead-based, err on the side of caution and follow the new EPA laws instituted in April 2010 regarding lead-paint abatement (www.epa.gov/lead). Builders, remodelers, and contractors must have RRP (renovation, repair, and painting) certification from the EPA to work with homeowners with lead issues. As a homeowner, it is important to review the new laws and work with a certified builder to ensure safe lead handling.

BRINGING IT ALL TOGETHER

Designing with salvaged material requires a certain amount of foresight and planning, and sometimes the details are forgotten. Keep in mind that if you are incorporating a vintage mantel, for example, designing around it to ensure that other aspects of the room are in harmony is important. If you purchased

antique doors, think about how the smaller doorways should match. Take the time to consider the entire integrated look; it will always pay off in the end.

PREPARING, INSTALLING, AND FINISHING

Often homeowners don't think about using salvaged wood in their construction or remodeling project because they're only picturing the wood in its natural color state. When homeowners want a sleek effect, they may not automatically think of using salvaged wood. However, different finishes produce a variety of looks, from sleek and modern to country quaint. The look you want will dictate the approach you take to preparing, installing, and finishing your salvaged wood.

▲ Brendan O'Reilly, the owner of Gristmill Builders, reviews a finishing job on an old salvaged door that is being turned into something new.

▸ Vintage beams, salvaged wood, and vintage wood and stained glass cabinet doors all add warmth to this exceptional winter hideaway.

Preparing

How to clean and prepare a piece of wood, as well as finish it, depends on many factors. The type of wood, the use of the wood, the color and character you are looking for—all of these make a difference. Many times something as simple as a light sanding is all you need to do to prepare the wood. Heavier sanding may be needed to achieve a cleaner, smoother piece of wood. For a rough-cut wall finish, straight edges and flat pieces (not bowed) are all that may matter if the wood is to be painted. Cleaning, planing, and sanding are all very important for a crisp, finished look. It is best to let the wood you've salvaged sit inside the space in which you plan to use it for a couple of weeks (or as long as it needs) to let it acclimate to the dry space—even vintage wood left outside has picked up a lot of moisture and will shrink after being in a warm, dry home, especially when the heat is on. It is much easier to prep the wood as a board than after it is in place as a floor, wall, or other structural element. Again, just as the kinds of woods available are nearly endless in variety, so too are the ways to prepare it.

Installing and Finishing the Wood

Finishing and installing your wood can be done in a number of different ways. The intended use, location of the wood, and your preferences will determine the type of sealer or finish, if any, you use. Your installer can help you determine the best look for you and any finishes needed to obtain it. Is there a wood

subfloor, concrete floor, radiant heat? What is the climate? Is there a lot of humidity in the house or is it a dry area? Answers to these questions will help determine the proper installation and finishes. Even nailing becomes an important issue—for example, using countersunk, square-head nails in wide pine boards is common when going for a more rustic look.

Examples of finishes and sealers include wax, shellac, nitrocellulose lacquer, conversion lacquer, linseed oil, tung oil, alkyd varnish, polyurethane varnish, water-based polyurethane, latex paints, whitewashing, and oil-varnish mixes. Each type of wood reacts differently to these finishes, and some finishes are more durable than others. An oil-rubbed finish may not hold up as well as water-based polyurethane, for example. It is worth doing some research on the best finish for your design and understanding how these finishes affect the wood.

Many architectural salvage shops and reclaimed-wood specialists have sample pieces, showrooms, or websites that show a variety of examples of finishes—how they look and how they work. This allows homeowners, designers, and builders to see the variety of ways the wood can be finished without having to create the pieces themselves. There are also many do-it-yourself websites, such as diy.com that give details on how to properly sand, stain, and finish your reclaimed wood.

Having a mudroom off the garage entrance is a practical idea. This one uses repurposed trim, with its original paint, from the home torn down on the same property. The bench uses salvaged dimensional lumber and the hooks were part of the electrical pieces in the old home. The floor with its quirky pattern of dots, is from an old bowling lane.

This kitchen addition, overlooking the 96-acre property, is filled with character and serves as an excellent example of the different ways salvaged wood can be used in a home. The cabinets (with the original pulls) are from a college chemistry lab, the window trim is salvaged trim boards, the floor is salvaged barn board, the upper cabinets where purchased at an antique shop (originally painted white), the cabinet at the end of the wall is an antique piece that now serves as a spice cupboard, and the beam along the ceiling was salvaged from an old barn. The tile along the windows was left over from another homeowner's project, the soapstone sink came from a neighbor's home, and the lighting is a vintage school light.

This master bathroom is an excellent example of how salvaged glass block can be used to bring natural light into a room while still providing privacy. The door and the cabinet, used instead of shelving, are both vintage.

Glass

Glass is an abundant material, and its uses go far beyond the architectural. For homeowners interested in salvage design, glass is an ideal material because no matter what its original shape, form, or purpose, it can be recycled again and again. It's also nonporous, nontoxic, and moisture- and stain-resistant—all traits favorable to green building.

This sunroom addition was created by a homeowner inspired by windows for sale on Craigslist. The windows let a tremendous amount of light into the small bungalow home, making it feel much larger than it is. The energy-efficient windows, salvaged tile, and salvaged woodstove tucked in the corner make this sunroom the homeowner's new favorite room in the house.

▸ Glass globes from lighting fixtures are in abundance at architectural salvage shops and rebuild centers. You can use them as what they were designed for or be creative and incorporate them in your home in a totally different way.

New glass is made from sand, soda ash, limestone, and varying additives, such as iron, chromium, cobalt, lead, alumina, and boron, which affect color, refraction, and thermal properties. Regardless of what it is made of, however, glass takes thousands and thousands of years to decompose. If not recycled, it can significantly contribute to the world's waste problem. According to the EPA, although recycling is on the rise, in the United States alone only about a third of all glass containers are recycled. Considering that all glass is recyclable, it is hard to see why we are not recycling 100% of it. What's more, this statistic doesn't include the glass from building-industry waste, such as old windows, shower stalls, and more.

The good news is that a growing number of companies are creating building materials composed of recycled glass, and building professionals and homeowners are using them. We are starting to see an upswing in the acceptance and use of recycled glass, which, in turn, creates jobs and saves homeowners (and the towns in which they live) money at the landfills. Whether you are salvaging a glass window and using it again in its current form or salvaging post-consumer and industrial glass waste and recycling it into a new product, the results are very much the same—100% recyclable, reusable, salvageable material for hundreds of home-design concepts.

This vintage wooden door with single-pane, older wavy glass provides a peek into the mudroom as well as a gorgeous view to the outside. It also allows southern light to flow into the entranceway and gives the homeowner the ability to close off the mudroom from the rest of the house.

There are also aesthetic and architectural benefits to using salvaged glass. Old glass (sometimes called "wavy" glass), with its bubbled texture, detailed stained glass, and vintage frosted doors from the 1950 have a special character that is hard to recreate with something brand new.

TYPES OF SALVAGED GLASS

For interior architectural purposes you can find salvaged glass in doors, window frames, or stand-alone as glass blocks or shower doors. There are also glass fixtures, hardware, and lighting. Look beyond their traditional uses and put together a design plan that not only incorporates these glass elements but enhances them.

Sheet Glass

This is the type of glass that was used in homes, factories, schools, and government buildings, built about a hundred years ago. You usually can tell if it is sheet glass because it has a bit of a distorted look and is not always completely flat. When purchasing older windows, you will find that they are made from window-grade sheet glass that has been glazed. This type of glass is easy to cut but more dangerous to work with because it breaks in large jagged pieces and is not energy-efficient. Therefore, these pieces of glass are best suited to older-window repair or interior projects.

Tempered or Laminated Glass

Tempered glass (also called "safety glass") is what most home-building glass products are made of today. Tempered glass has been treated to be four to five times stronger than regular sheet glass. It also goes through an entirely different process before it is even treated. Tempered glass is used when contact to people is high, such as in a house. Windows, doors, showers, furniture, countertops—all these use tempered glass, which will shatter into thousands of pieces if broken rather than into sharp-edged fragments. Laminated glass does not shatter and the benefit of this type of glass is that it can be cut. Building code laws require tempered or laminated glass in some locations in the home, such as in bathroom shower. It is important to know the building codes to ensure you are using the right type of salvaged glass.

Stained Glass

The abundance and variety of stained glass pieces becomes apparent when you visit an architectural salvage shop, antique shop, or antiques market. Found in all shapes, sizes, and colors, stained glass can add a sense of drama with a lively, colorful piece or a

This vintage stained glass window, discovered at a salvage shop, separates a home office from the rest of the house, affording privacy and light.

▲ This small stained-glass piece in the master bedroom not only adds a design element but also brings natural light from the bedroom into the hallway. At night, the vintage light fixture in the hall adds a warm glow to the bedroom, serving as a nightlight for the room.

▶ A salvaged stained glass piece was used in this upper cabinet, creating a header above the island as well as a light fixture. It also visually divides the kitchen from the living room, while keeping it an open space.

DESIGN TIP

Old salvaged windows aren't usually as energy-efficient as modern glass panes, making them better for use as interior windows or dividers. Sacrificing energy efficiency to use salvaged glass for exterior windows doesn't make sense—unless you prepare it with an energy panel. Today's window products are built to keep homes warm in the winter and cool in the summer. Many manufacturers of exterior windows now use up to 50% recycled glass, allowing energy-efficiency and salvaged material to coexist.

calm, stately feel with a piece that has more textures than colors. They can be used as cabinet doors, as visual separations for rooms, or even as privacy windows. Don't let a bowed stained glass piece or even one with a crack scare you away. They are usually easy to repair. Sometimes it can be as simple as placing clear epoxy cement over a cracked piece or even adding a little bit of putty to a lead edge to stabilize it. Stained glass pieces are more for visual effect than structural use. Stable stained glass is fine for cabinet doors or windows but should not be used in a location that gets a lot of movement or carries a lot of load. If you do decide to use a piece on an exterior wall, place an energy panel on the outside to create an insulated space and to keep the elements off the piece, ensuring the window is air-tight and energy-efficient.

▲ Glass block can be used in almost every style of home—Arts and Crafts, modern, minimalist, cottage. They can be used for bathroom shower stalls, for exterior walls to provide privacy, and even for backsplashes or other design elements. Styles vary. Some have a wavy look; some have a rain-splatter look. When you find glass block in more than one location, try to match up the pattern on the block.

▸ The bubble-pattern glass block used in the bathroom of this seaside cottage allows light to enter through the window in the shower while still giving the bather privacy. Recycled glass tiles create a colorful, welcoming pattern above salvaged wainscoting that was painted white.

Glass Blocks

Salvaged glass block is a perfect alternative material for non-load-bearing walls and internal windows—it partitions spaces for privacy but still allows natural light to pass through. Glass block is an excellent choice for an area in the home that needs a structural element as well as privacy and a design element. It's also a low-maintenance product that can be installed much the same way bricks are, with a grout or even a type of glue, clear silicone, or epoxy, depending on the location and use.

Crushed Glass

Crushed salvaged glass, with its endless color variations and ability to be formed into different shapes and sizes, is a material of many talents. In its recycled form it can be used to create tiles, sinks, countertops, light fixtures, energy-efficient windows, and windowsills. It can even serve as an aggregate in a concrete mix.

Terrazzo

In addition to being a municipality in Italy, terrazzo has over fifteen definitions, the most basic of which refers to flooring, walls, and other structures that have marble, quartz, or stone chips (a material that is mined) embedded in cement or other resinous mixture and then polished. The marble or stone chips are the aggregate in the mixture—the terrazzo, so to speak. Today, with an increased interest in green building, 100% recycled-glass terrazzo is a popular salvaged material used in a variety of design concepts, from flooring to countertops, bathroom sinks, tiles, and more. In terms of size, terrazzo glass pieces can range from tiny powder-sized granules to pieces the size of a coin. A countertop made from powder-fine glass terrazzo can look just like natural stone; only the homeowner will know the difference. If larger-sized glass pieces are used, it can be much more noticeable, as large chunks of the terrazzo will be scattered throughout the countertop. The way in which you choose to use terrazzo completely depends on the look and style you're going for and the percentage of recycled glass your want in your finished product.

This countertop is 100% recycled from the same type and source of glass. Because the counter is large—3½ x 8 feet—the glass was created in layers that were then stacked onto each other.

Salvaged glass terrazzo can be used in one of three ways: (1) as a large, single piece, such as an entire countertop or vessel (sink), (2) as smaller pieces, such as tile, where the variety of shapes, colors, and sizes is wider, and (3) as a material that can be crushed and then mixed with cement, concrete, or resin to create countertops, floors, or even tiles for bathrooms and backsplashes.

Tiles were made from salvaged glass. There are hundreds of natural glass colors and shapes to choose from when using salvaged glass. Green bottles, clear bottles, industrial glass waste, natural dies mixed with glass—these are just a few of the ways glass can get its color. Subway tiles, small squares, and even circles are some fun shapes to consider for your salvaged glass design.

◂ This island countertop shows salvaged glass used in two different ways. The upper part of the island—the bar area—is concrete mixed with an aggregate made of small, pebble-sized glass. The glass flecks give a beautiful design element to the piece. The lower part of the island was made with salvaged glass crushed into a fine powder and then mixed into concrete, giving the counter a more stonelike look. This contemporary kitchen also uses additional green products, making it an inspired contemporary space.

DESIGN TIP

Many types of terrazzo systems exist. When researching terrazzo, look for forms that use 75 to 100% postconsumer or postindustrial glass and a binding substance (e.g., cement) that is nontoxic and can handle as much as 75% glass aggregate.

POSSIBLE USES

As you design your home think about locations where you can add salvage or recycled glass elements. If you are considering finishing a basement and adding bedrooms to it, can the doors be salvaged with frosted glass to add more light while maintaining privacy? In place of shower tile, why not use tiered glass block or add a special glass light fixture to brighten up a bathroom? Whatever its shape or form, glass adds a great deal of style to any home.

◂ This bathroom tub surround is another example of how recycled glass can be used. The crushed glass in the concrete was from glass materials found in a condemned home that was on the property before the new house was constructed, as well as the salvaged pieces of wood used as trim work.

Glass Windows and Doors

French diamond window panes with fine details, etched glass doors, and antique stained glass windows are all examples of glass work that is hard to find in today's products. Although these forms of glass are not recommended for external use (except for seasonal homes that do not have heating or air-conditioning systems), they are perfect for interior design concepts. Consider using glass as an alternative to a wall to separate rooms, or position a window in an interior room to allow natural light to shine through. Use glass for pantry doors or in French doors to a sunroom. These are all excellent ways to incorporate salvaged glass windows and doors into a home.

Tile

The ranges of design concepts using salvaged glass tiles are endless. A rainbow display, a cool glassy green, even a bold black—any color, size, shape, or style can be achieved using 100% recycled glass tile. Many recycle glass companies will create custom colors and shapes for their clients.

▲ This detail of a guest bathroom at a seaside home shows a unique recycled glass tile design, as well as salvaged beadboard, door trim, and door made from logs salvaged from a nearby river.

◀ Vintage doors with large glass panes allow for light to flow into this bedroom while cutting out noise and creating a unique design for a private master-suite space.

Countertops

Like most products that contain glass, salvaged glass countertops consist of either 100% recycled glass with no binding agent or a large percentage of recycled glass with a small percentage of binder (such as cement or an epoxy). It is very difficult to create countertops out of 100% salvaged glass, and only a few companies do it. Both options are very eco-friendly, especially if there is low VOC (volatile organic compounds) resin usage—which basically means it is low in toxic compounds. Glass countertops are as sturdy as any stone counterpart. However, just like with stone, it is best to avoid dropping something large and heavy on them.

◂ Recycled, reflective black glass looks almost silver when the sunlight shines on it. Its rich color against the modern features of the kitchen adds elegance to the space.

▾ This remodeled kitchen reflects simple, elegant style. The salvaged glass raised counter above the main countertop is not only a conversation piece but also makes the space feel larger. The natural color of the glass, a greenish hue, blends well with the elegance of the darker wood and metal brackets.

Backsplashes

Kitchen backsplashes are where many homeowners get creative and use interesting glass shapes and colors, or even back-light the glass. Flat panels of recycled glass will give a kitchen a clean, modern style; exciting, bold colors and shapes can give a kitchen a more fun, whimsical, casual feeling.

Interior Windows and Doors

Natural light is an important aspect of all home designs, and salvaged glass windows or doors, as mentioned earlier, can allow for separation of space while maintaining a good flow of light. Another way to add character to your design

◂ This circular, salvaged glass backsplash proves that tiles don't have to be traditionally shaped. The homeowner hand-placed the tiles to create an exceptionally fun, unique look for her kitchen.

▾ These salvage vintage doors add a dramatic entrance to a modern kitchen. Left open on a barn slide against the red wall, it becomes artwork for the space as well.

▲ Using salvaged aluminum and vases already owned by the homeowner, an artisan-based company created this unique lighting fixture for the stairwell to the media room and office.

is by incorporating artistic glass, such as salvaged stained glass windows, mirrors, or antique wooden doors with glass panels in them.

Lighting

Old glass globes, etched glass, and glass shades that cover light fixtures can be used again for new projects, and other glass objects, such as bottles or jars, can be repurposed into creative lighting concepts. Chapter 5 goes into detail about the many options available for lighting.

Hardware

Don't forget about the unique options available with glass hardware. Vintage doorknobs or pulls made of salvaged glass are an easy way to incorporate salvaged glass into a home design. There are also many companies that make more modern or contemporary 100% recycled glass knobs and pulls.

◀ These glass doorknobs at an architectural shop can be used on doors, as draw pulls, or even as hooks for coats. The salvaged glass doorknobs are common glass pieces you can find at shops or online.

▲ Medicine cabinets are easy to find. Be creative—line them up along the wall as cabinets.

This bathroom illustration features salvaged glass block for a step-in shower with salvaged concrete with glass aggregate. The stained-glass piece hanging in front of the glass gives a bit more privacy as well as a pop of color to the room. A vintage sink supported by legs lets the salvaged painted wood floors stand out and makes the room look bigger. A floor color that matches one of the colors in the stained-glass piece and a funky salvaged mirror and wall sconce would round it all off.

Bathrooms

When putting your design plans together, bathrooms are a smart place to consider integrating salvaged glass. Because it is nonporous, glass is especially well-suited to the bathroom. Smooth, recycled-glass-and-concrete floors, recycled glass tiles, salvaged glass blocks, tempered-glass shower panels, glass hardware, and recycled mirrors—an entire bathroom can be designed with salvaged glass.

These vintage etched glass doors make a grand entrance to the master closet and bathroom. Old grain bins from a general store serve as the closet drawers. The flooring is salvaged barn board that has been planed and sealed.

DESIGN TIP

Large glassmaking manufacturers are on the decline in the U.S., meaning that much of today's new glass is imported. This results not only in a large energy and environmental expenditure but an economic one as well. An easy way to support our local businesses (and therefore, our communities), is to buy salvaged-glass products. A recent upswing in the number of small-shop artisan glassmakers who work solely with salvaged pieces makes this easy to do. Take full advantage of their knowledge and skill, especially when it comes to determining the best use of salvaged glass and the installation procedures.

▸ Simple details, like adding a vintage cabinet door with wavy glass, can change a design style dramatically. Glass cabinet doors in a kitchen add depth to the room and can show off attractive dishware.

STRUCTURAL ELEMENTS TO CONSIDER

Different types of glass are used for different purposes. Understanding building codes when it comes to the use of glass in the home will help when you're searching for the perfect salvaged glass pieces.

All salvaged glass you might use should be checked for structural integrity, particularly old windows, stained glass, and glass block. Old windows tend to have cracked or missing chalking around the glass that can be repaired, removed completely, or rechalked. Stained glass can be difficult to work with if it does not have a structural frame around it. Many homeowners affix a piece of clear salvaged glass to one or both sides to keep the stained glass from bowing if it is not stable. Glass block should be checked for cracks and the old chalking or glues need to be completely removed before reassembling. Small cracks in glass or the surrounding wood frames are easy to fix and if the piece is just right for the design project, repairs should be seriously considered.

CHALLENGES WITH GLASS

Glass can be dangerous to work with. It is important that you seek out a professional or someone who has experience with the type of glass you are working with. Regular glass is easy to score and cut with a straightedge (with gloves and eye protection) but tempered glass cannot be cut with a normal glass cutter; it needs to be cut by a professional. And if glass is cut wrong it can easily break or shatter. Many homeowners are turning to laminate glass because it

▸ This striking dining room in a converted warehouse that now serves as a home, studio, and office for a sculptor is filled with the homeowner's work. The table was once a branch of a big leaf maple that had fallen during a storm and was lying in someone's front yard (he knocked on the door and asked if he could have it). As a sculptor, he let the tree's natural form and live edge speak for the table. The windows above the doors to his workshop were salvaged from a courthouse before it was torn down. They allow natural light to flow into the workshop from the skylights in the dining area. The floors are salvaged pieces of plywood cut to form patterns (see Chapter 1).

can be cut and meets code in many home locations. Understanding what type of glass the salvaged pieces are made of and where it can be used in the home project is important, especially if you want to pass the building inspection at the end of it.

FINISHES, SEALING, AND INSTALLATION

Old window sashes may need a sealer on the wood to keep it from chipping (remember lead-paint issues discussed in Chapter 1). The glass may be loose and need to be stabilized with a clear caulking (or silicone) around the edge of the glass and wood. It is something that should be done as a precaution anyway.

When working with glass block you need to remove all the old adhesives and make sure the surface is clean before installation. If the glass block will be in a structural location, or part of an outside wall, check each block carefully for cracks or chips. These can be sealed after installation but it is best to correct any problems before placing them.

Another way to stabilize a glass piece or window is to add a wood frame around it. If it already has one, add a piece of trim or layer the wood-frame pieces.

GLASS WITH BINDER

The binder—or binding agent—used with salvaged glass terrazzo is usually a cement or resin-based product, and the aggregate is the glass itself. Concrete (a cement-based binder) or nontoxic binders are the best choices. Petroleum-based or chemical polyester binders should be avoided.

The type and style of glass you choose will determine the type of finish and installation needed. For example, you will need to let your counter cure for about a month before you seal it. The type of sealer (or combination of sealers) you use will depend on the materials you used and the type of finish you want, especially if you are using larger chunks of glass. If you're using finely crushed glass, you can go with a slightly polished or honed appearance to make the glass counters look almost exactly like natural stone, with a warm, organic feel. When salvaged crushed glass is combined with a concrete mixer, a sealer will be necessary. The manufacturer will usually provide this and give instructions for further maintenance and sealing.

▲ This guest-bathroom concrete countertop, made with recycled glass, serves as the top of a custom-made salvaged wood vanity. The salvaged vintage glass wall sconces flank the sides of a vintage glass mirror. The glass pulls on the vanity are salvaged doorknobs.

▶ This cozy window seat combines modern tempered-glass windows with a salvaged stained-glass piece that was sealed with an energy panel of clear glass on the outside of the home.

DESIGN TIP

Separating rooms without walls by salvaged-glass pieces is an exceptional way to allow natural light into the spaces while giving the illusion of a wall. Be creative—hang a variety of old windows together with chains, get a custom piece made from recycled tiles, place a stained-glass piece in your bathroom wall or even as a transom above your entranceway door. Visit an architectural salvage shop and think about the ways in which you can use their glass pieces.

This master bathroom in a seaside home highlights a vintage cast-iron tub with enamel coating. The homeowner stripped the metal base and loved the color so much that she decided not to paint it. The glass block window is another great example of where salvaged glass block can be used.

Metal

Metal can be salvaged in two different ways: It can be repurposed, such as an old iron gate reused as a decorative half door, or it can be melted down (recycled) and reused in a different form, like copper shreds melted down and made into drawer pulls. Both ways of reusing this versatile material are equally effective.

Metal cabinets in a marble-filled bathroom with a vintage door and metal faceplate make a striking contrast that works very well.

The weight of a material often drives up the cost of disposal, and metal, whether it is scrap, appliances, screens, or plumbing, is usually heavy, making it costly to get rid of. Repurposing and recycling metal helps mitigate these costs and eases the strain on our landfills.

Shipping containers, cast-iron radiators, appliances, nails, screens, doors, aluminum cans, and copper piping are just a few of the metal items that are commonly recycled and reused. Still, a significant amount of metal that could be recycled or sold as scrap continues to fall into construction-site dumpsters. So, whether you are looking for a Victorian radiator, a 1950s stove, a country-style drawer pull, or a modern, sleek light fixture, your chances of finding it at a salvage shop are good.

Companies that specialize in using 100% salvaged metal to create new products—such as fixtures, lights, and hardware—are still pretty new and hard to come by; homeowners and builders may have to do a little research to find these suppliers. Look locally for a small company that specializes in recycled metal, or ask a local metal shop where you can find someone to fabric a custom piece for you. As with wood, the more local the supplier the better, as transporting heavy metal pieces takes a toll on environmental and energy resources.

Salvaged metal grates, metal hardware, and light fixtures are easy to come by at architectural and recycle shops. Metal tables, shelving, or cabinets can be found at office-supplies stores, restaurant salvage shops, or even university warehouses. Plan ahead to find the right piece before the design process is finished. It is much easier to work around a piece than to try to incorporate one after the design has been completed.

Make a list of all the locations where you plan to use metal in your design. Salvaged or recycled hardware, fixtures, lighting, grates, vents, and shelving can add style to all the functional parts of your home.

LEED CREDITS

According to LEED (Leadership in Energy and Environmental Design) green-building guidelines, steel is the only material for which LEED allows you to claim a default of 25% recycled content. It is usually better to ascertain the exact amount of recycled content and how the steel was made for more credits. There are numerous LEED credits available for steel and other metals, so it is important to look through their guidelines to learn more. For example, metal roofs can contribute to LEED credits.

TYPES OF SALVAGED METAL

Today's new homes and renovation projects are adding innovative salvaged designs using a range of metals, which are no longer limited to commercial or industrial buildings. Modern, classic, and "cottage" styles can all be achieved by incorporating interesting salvage and recycled metals.

Evaluating a salvaged metal sink at a recycle center.

Steel

When people think about salvage materials, beautiful, old wood flooring or unique architectural pieces often come to mind first, but the most commonly salvaged material in North America is, in fact, a metal—steel, to be exact. Today's "new" steel has a minimum of 25% postconsumer, recycled material, and most of the time it has even more than that. Electric arc furnace (EAF) steel (a batch-melting process that makes molten steel), typically used in beams, columns, and angle iron, can contain up 70% recycled material. So, whether intentionally or not, when you use steel in your projects, you are already using partially salvaged materials. Even metal shipping containers are becoming more and more popular around the world, salvaged for use in homes, as cottages or freestanding office or studio spaces, and as storage space. In Europe, entire high-rise complexes are being made from shipping containers. Realistically, the average home design or remodeling project will not include a steel shipping container, but it can easily incorporate salvaged metal appliances, sinks, hardware, countertops, and more—everyday items that can be found at the local recycle centers or architectural salvage shops.

▲ This modern home shows how exposed steel can be used as part of the design aesthetic. The wood beams in this home were also salvaged.

▸ Screens, usually thrown in a dumpster during a construction project, are an excellent example of how seemingly unusable items can be used again. These items are picked up from the rebuild center and used by an artisan-based company to create recycled aluminum sinks, lighting fixtures, and hardware.

▸▸ The hardware on these custom built cabinets was made from the metal recycled from the screens in the photo above. Metal hardware can be older vintage pieces, salvaged hardware, or modern designer pieces made from recycled metal such as these.

Aluminum

Aluminum can be salvaged from a number of items, including windows, doors, containers, appliances, and even cars. Ground into small pieces and melted down, it is pressed into sheets at varying thicknesses, depending on the end product. Products made out of recycled aluminum range from items as large as roofing to those as small as drawer pulls.

Using salvaged aluminum that has been recycled into something new is a particularly green design choice because the material can be recycled indefinitely. Flat-rolled aluminum products (roofing is one example) can have up to 85% recycled content. They also last much longer than most nonmetal products, can be 100% recycled at the end of a useful life, are extremely fire-resistant, and have a low life-cycle cost (few repair issues). When used as roofing, aluminum can be placed right over the old roof—saving removal and disposal costs. Many homeowners think of metal as conducting heat and don't consider using it in their homes, but aluminum tiles on the floors can actually help keep the temperature in a home even. Recycling aluminum consumes about 95% less energy than converting bauxite (the raw material) into new aluminum, making salvaging it seem like an even better idea.

Copper

The value of copper has risen significantly, so you rarely see copper sitting in a dumpster. For this reason, copper has also become a highly sought-after recycled metal. Sheets of salvaged copper—perfect for lighting, accents, edging for fireplaces, flashing, roofing, counter-

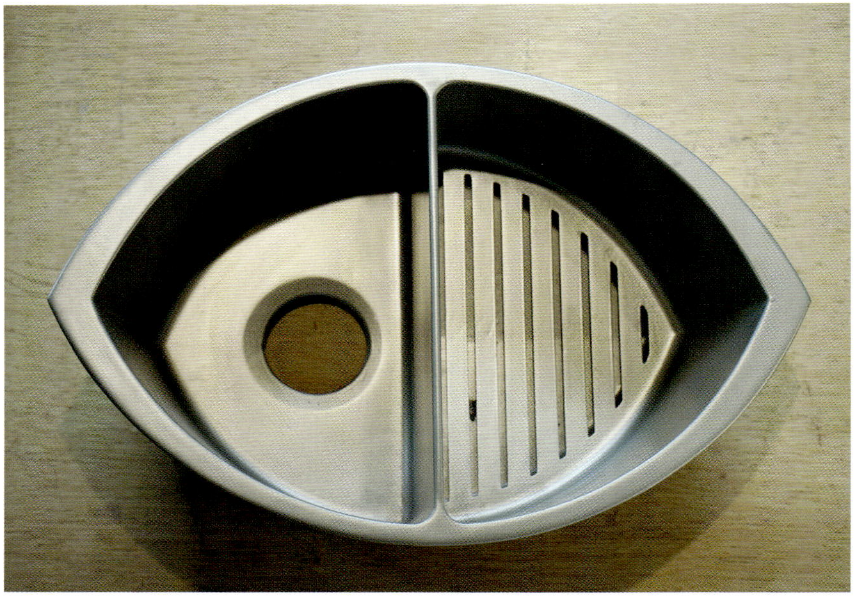

▲ Modern lighting fixtures combine salvaged metal and energy-efficient bulbs, showing that salvaged material does not need to look old, country, or rustic.

▶ This sink with its own built-in drain board is made from salvaged metal that was melted down and reformed into a new product. You can find 100% recycled products with a little bit of research, and many artisan-based companies can make custom products.

tops, and backsplashes—can be found at recycle centers, architectural salvage shops, or metal shops. You can even use recycled copper piping for island foot rests or to hang pots and pans. Most copper products today are made with 75% recycled-copper content, but companies offering 100% recycled-copper products can be found with a little research.

Many metals, like stainless steel and aluminum, do not readily oxidize and therefore do not need to be finished or sealed. Copper, however, is not one of them—it change colors and patina if not sealed with spray lacquer to prevent oxygen from reaching the surface. That said, the patina of unsealed copper can be remarkably beautiful, especially for a standing-seam copper roof. (A standing-seam roof is one with ridges along its panels.) Copper standing seam starts out bright copper, then changes into a green color, and then slowly develops a darker, browner patina. Seeing samples of copper as it ages will help you decide if it is the right look for your home design. If you do decide to go with copper roofing, be prepared for its cost, which is high but worth it if you want a roof that will last a lifetime and patina beautifully.

Brass, Chrome, and Nickel

Many lighting and hardware fixtures are made of (or plated in) brass, chrome, or nickel. Usually you can tell the difference between these metals by their colors. Brass is a reddish gold color, chrome is a shiny silver color, and nickel is a dull silver-grayish color (or shiny, if polished). Brass is usually the most common and affordable of these three metals, but all three are easy to find.

▸ Metal bowls, clocks, and other unique pieces are in abundance, and how they are used is limited only to your imagination. This copper candy bowl, probably once used to make fudge, was left to patina in its natural state and then used as a second sink in this farmhouse kitchen. The 17-foot-long counter in which it is set is from an old general store.

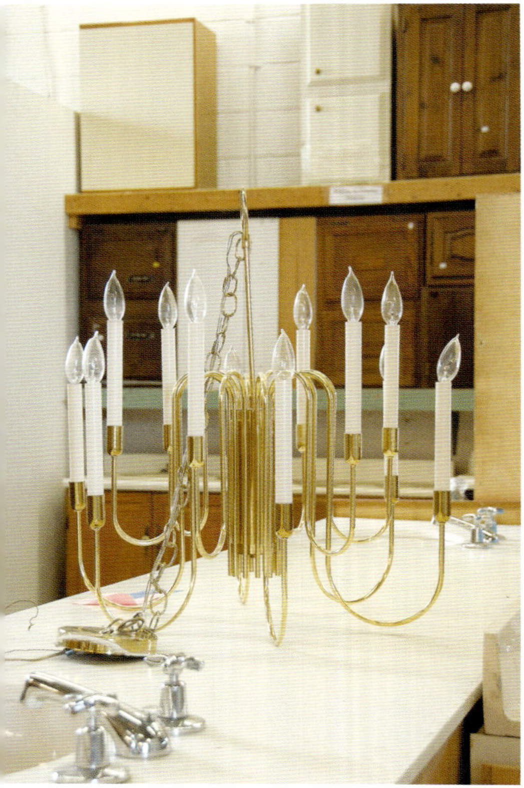

▲ Hundreds of brass chandeliers from the 1970s and 1980s can be found at recycle centers. These affordable ceiling fixtures can often be used as is and the wiring rarely needs to be replaced. Check to see if the lighting piece works before you make any adjustments to it. Sometimes a bulb has broken off or is rusted into place. Carefully remove it and check each bulb slot to make sure they all work.

▶ After being checked to make sure all the bulb slots were in working order, the lighting fixture here was lightly sanded and painted white. The plastic pieces below the bulbs were glittered, vintage teardrop crystals were added, and the clear glass bulbs were replaced with textured ones. With a little bit of work, this light fixture took on a whole new look.

Cast Iron and Wrought Iron

Cast iron and wrought iron may look similar, but they are manufactured differently. Tools are used to give wrought iron its form, and cast iron is metal that has been poured into a mold and then allowed to cool and harden. Old cast-iron grates, radiators, tubs, and enamel-coated sinks can be found in abundance at salvage and recycle shops. During the turn of the nineteenth century, cast iron was much more affordable than porcelain, and fixtures made from a variety of molds became a household staple. Double sinks with drain boards, pedestal

▲ An architectural salvage warehouse can hold a variety of metal objects—tubs, sinks, hardware, lighting, fixtures, and more. Take your time to look through these shops and try to picture the pieces in their "after" phase in your design.

sinks with rounded edges, soaker tubs—these are just a few of the cast-iron salvage selections available. These items are heavy, solid pieces that lend a feeling of permanence to any design. They add character to any room and can be used in conjunction with other salvaged fixtures, such as brass faucets.

SALVAGED METAL PIECES

Old tin ceilings, luggage racks from train cars, cast-iron sewing stands, iron gates, and floor grates are just a few of the unique salvaged metal pieces that can be incorporated into the design concept of any home. Tin ceiling materials can be placed on a wall behind a wood stove—or even back on the ceiling. Old iron garden gates can be hung above a stove or island for pots and pans. Floor grates are perfect for entranceways, and cast-iron water faucets from a school can be used in mudroom for the kids after a hot day in the summer sun.

RECYCLED METAL PRODUCTS

When you can't find exactly what you are looking for in salvaged metal, look for companies that specialize in using salvaged metal pieces to create 100% recycled metal products—hardware, sinks, tiles, roofing, flooring, and so on. As mentioned earlier, many of these companies will even make custom pieces to order.

▲ At the end of this bar is an old tractor wheel and plow salvaged from a local farm. The barn board on the bar, as well as the footstool, which is an old barn-door sliding rail, are also salvaged pieces.

◀ This tub was moved from another part of the home during renovation. The homeowners painted the exposed metal on the bottom with white paint. They left the enamel in its original condition. The freestanding cupboard was found in a relative's barn, unused. The window curtain (an old skirt) brings in a bit of color.

◂ Metal lockers from a college dormitory (bought at a college warehouse sale) really make a statement in this entranceway. The vintage stools are also from a warehouse sale. Many colleges and hotels have their own warehouses that sell materials and pieces they have removed from their dormitories, labs, classrooms, and guestrooms. The counter is a piece of salvaged soapstone and the red slates are retail wall board for hooks, salvaged from a retail shop. Together, these salvaged pieces make for a fun and welcoming space for this busy snowboarding family.

DESIGN TIP

The average three-bedroom home has about 75 to 150 drawer pulls, doorknobs, hinges, towel racks, and fixtures. Multiply that by the millions of households in the U.S. alone, and you have a lot of fixtures to consider. Whatever the style—modern, simple, Victorian, cottage—salvaged or 100% recycled hardware is available to fit your design needs. Visit salvage or recycle centers to get a feel for what they have and their pricing. If you are using older doors, try glass or bronze knobs. Simple chrome pulls from a more recent era will probably be better for a more modern design. Going for a totally eclectic look? Find a different piece of hardware for every door, cabinet, and closet you have! These are just a few examples of the thousands of choices.

This illustration shows that putting together a modern, convenient kitchen can be as simple as purchasing used stainless-steel restaurant tables and pendant lights, some salvaged metal brackets, an old laundry sink (concrete, soapstone, or slate), and some old wooden boards for shelves. All of these salvaged materials can be found at a very affordable price.

POSSIBLE USES

Before considering how best to use salvaged metal in your home design, get a basic understanding of what metals are available and how they can be used structurally. The assumption is that metal is tough, cold material that will create a "chilly" space, but not so! Metals come in all shapes, sizes, and densities; it's also quite malleable and can therefore be manipulated to fit your particular needs. If you find just the right cut, you can also use an entire piece of old metal in your home, like putting salvaged metal along the entire living-room wall for a unique design statement.

Countertops and Islands

Restaurant suppliers often carry used stainless-steel tables that can be made into an island or even a kitchen countertop. This is a very affordable alternative to built-in islands or counters with cabinets, as many of these metal tables have

This countertop is a piece of sheet metal that the homeowner had shaped to fit the counter and sink. The salvaged cast-iron, enamel-coated sink—from an industrial building that was being deconstructed—gives this compact kitchen a sense of spaciousness. The simplicity of the design around it allows the piece to be the architectural focal point, helping control costs. The whimsical vintage skateboard stands out as part of the pendant light against the painted salvaged plywood ceiling and the salvaged dimensional-lumber trusses. The drawer pulls are made from pieces of salvaged sheet metal that the owner bent to into an L shape. The drawers are made from salvaged decking.

lower metal shelves as well. It can also give a kitchen an urban, industrial, modern feel. Another option is to have pieces of copper soldered or brazed together to form a countertop. Salvaged or recycled stainless steel, brass, or aluminum sheets or tiles are also great countertop materials; all can easily be cut or assembled to fit the dimensions of the project.

Sinks and Tubs

A variety of options exist when it comes to using salvaged metal in a sink or bathroom tub. Consider salvaged enameled cast iron, salvaged stainless steel, or even a new sink made from recycled metals. Some homeowners get creative and turn other metal objects, like metal colanders into special sinks for vegetable cutting and washing. Colored enamel finishes on cast iron are becoming popular again, allowing even more creativity in the design. They can even be recolored to match your needs.

Tile

Tiles made from 100% recycled metal have become very urban chic. Tiles come in many different sizes, colors, and finishes, and they can be used in a variety of projects, including backsplashes for kitchens and bathrooms and even flooring.

Hardware

Like salvaged glass hardware, metal hardware—whether it is a vintage drawer pull or a recycled modern piece—is an easy way to add character to the cabinetry and doors of a home. And it's easy to find lots of different pieces—back plates, knobs, hinges, strike plates, catches, keyhole escutcheons, and more. If you like the piece but don't care for the finish, you can have the piece rechromed, galvanized, or even powder-coated by a professional, or you can

◂ Enameled metal pieces in an array of colors are in abundance at recycle centers and architectural salvage shops. Powder blue for a seaside seasonal cottage, red for a whimsical bathroom, and emerald green for a richer look are just a few of the possibilities. If you like the shape, structure, or brand of a salvaged metal piece but not the enamel color, you can have the enamel redone by a professional.

▴ These red sinks, found at an architectural salvage shop, blend well with an antique mirror and the homeowner's handmade tile, also a great example of modern fixtures reused.

A simple vintage metal knob and faceplate on a vintage door are all this room needs. Against the textured wall, the door and the knob are an exceptional example of how elegant a design with detailed salvaged materials can be.

simply polish or sand it and leave as is or use a spray enamel paint to give it color—even a metal color. You can mix and match more modern brass or metal pieces or find matching antique hardware sets with exceptional details and designs—gems for your doors. Antique hardware is not necessarily designed to

DESIGN TIP

A simple way to repurpose your own hardware is to change the color or even the actual metal coating. A metal shop can transform a brass fixture by plating it with chrome (for a shiny, silver look) or galvanizing it (for a more flat, rustic look). Another affordable change is to paint it a metal color (use a metal paint spray) or even paint on a fun pattern or design and seal it with a clear epoxy.

▲ The hardware above was sanded and sprayed with a black metal paint.

◀ Spend some time determining how many pulls and knobs you need so you'll be ready to buy when you see them. Matching hardware doesn't last long at a recycle center.

▼ The drawer pulls below were painted with a matte silver metal to give them a galvanized look.

See how these old pieces of metal have been stained and transformed into a unique banister or railing. You can get very creative when working with salvaged metal.

be airtight, especially if it has a skeleton key, so understand how the mechanics work before you decide to attach the piece to your door, especially an exterior door.

Fixtures

Faucets and lighting fixtures are two common examples of salvaged metal products. (See Chapter 5 for a discussion on lighting.) Many homeowners shy away from older faucets, but many of these older fixtures have beautiful details and can be adjusted to fit new appliances if necessary. There are hundreds of shapes and sizes of old fixtures. This variety makes them fun to design with but difficult to work with if they don't match today's standard sizes. Adjustment pieces made need to be added. If you fall in love with an antique fixture, learn all there is to know about it and find a plumber who knows how to work with older pieces.

If you are using older fixtures for plumbing, make sure they don't have lead inside them (look for a dark-gray soft metal inside). Fixtures with lead should not be used for drinking water. You may, however, be able to alter the piece to make it usable. For example, some old fixtures with copper piping are soldered together with lead-based solder. The solder should be removed before the rest of the metal pieces are used. This is a good time to

▲ Sometimes all a salvaged fixture needs is a good polishing. Cleaned up, the salvaged pieces here gleam as they await their new owners.

seek out a professional, especially with the new lead laws and the steps that need to be followed to remove lead from your home.

Shelving, Pot Racks, and Storage

Salvaged metal brackets to support shelves are a simple, affordable way to green up your home by using less building material than built-in cabinetry would have. Many homeowners also use decorative metal pieces as structural elements in their home design. A structurally sound recycled metal rack hanging over the island or stove adds a tremendous amount of character to the busiest room in the house. Salvaged metal cabinets are often great (and affordable) storage solutions for a mudroom, pantry, office, or bathroom. Metal medicine cabinets are easy to find, and the mirrors in them are usually in great shape. The metal around the edges can be refinished if necessary.

Copper contains a large percentage of recycled material. Add a unique salvaged piece and you have a one-of-a-kind bar, counter, and light fixture.

Snow and Sand Walk-Off Grates

These are very popular in the Northeast, where the long winter and mud season tend to bring a lot of water and dirt into a home. A salvaged metal grate in the decking of your entranceway allows you to stamp off snow and mud (which falls through the grate) before you go inside. These grates also add a decorative design element to the entry of the home. Beach houses (with lots of sandy feet) are another great place for entryway grates. These grates are available new, but old ones have a lot of character and, of course, aren't using up energy to manufacture. Another alternative is to find a company that makes new grates out of recycled metal.

Salvaged floor grates can also be used for floor heating vents or along a wall for heating, speaker, or vent cover. Look for grates that have a wide lip around them and measure twice to make sure the hole you cut is the right size. When using a grate on a floor surface, it is a good idea to recess the grate into the surface and screw it down. This helps prevent tripping over it.

Roofs and Exteriors

One of the primary ways scrap metal is used is for roofing. There are many benefits to using metal roofs. First, the recycle content of metal roofs is very high, ranging from 75% in a copper roof to 85% in an aluminum roof. Second, they last much longer than most roofing material and are lightweight enough to be placed directly over an old roof, saving money on removal and disposal of the old material. Third, as mentioned earlier, they are extremely fire-resistant, have a low life-cycle cost (few repair issues), and are energy-efficient (a heat insulator). Also, unlike asphalt roofing, a metal roof, if removed, can be salvaged and recycled all over again if necessary. One of the drawbacks of using a metal roof is that many homeowners find them louder than a traditional asphalt or stone roof. If the metal roof is not sealed with a coating it can rust, but most

A salvaged piece of metal used as a pot rack can work well in both large and small spaces. This kitchen also uses salvaged wood that was repurposed from the same room (it had served as ceiling joists running in a different direction). The flooring in the room was repurposed from the attic, and the wide pine wall panels were from another location in the home.

▸ With their different shapes, sizes, and details, these metal grates at an architectural salvage warehouse are like artwork. They can be used as heating vents, speaker frames, or metal grates for floors.

▾ Perfect for an entranceway, older metal grates can be painted to make them look new. This metal grate at a lakefront home in the Northeast sees lots of use and is helpful in removing both snow and sand on shoes and feet.

▸▸ Aluminum siding made from leftover scrap metal and then bent to create a shingle look was used on the side of this rebuilding-material center. A great example of how creative you can get with metal.

roof companies use metal that is properly sealed, so this is not usually a concern. Many homeowners are using salvaged metal for exterior walls as well—a modern entranceway with salvaged copper, galvanized metal sheets, or even shingles can make a unique design statement.

Wall and Ceiling Coverings

Old tin ceilings, galvanized metal sheets, or recycled tin pieces can be used as a wall covering, or placed back up as a ceiling in a manner similar to older Victorian homes. They can even be used as heat shields behind woodstoves, or placed on the front of cabinet doors, around the sides of an island, or even in a shower.

Appliances

It is impossible to have a chapter on metal without touching on salvaged appliances. With new Energy Star-rated appliances that significantly cut down on energy usage, it is sometimes hard to fathom looking for older or second-hand appliances, but there are a few reasons homeowners still consider them. First, the up-front cost can be much more affordable. Second, older appliances may be more appropriate for historic restorations or for cottage-style second homes in which the appliances get little use. Third, the look of salvaged appliances may better fit the design. Although these are all good reasons, it is important to try to use salvaged appliances only as accent pieces or in a second home where they are not often used, because most older electric appliances can't be made more

▲ During renovation the owner of this home wanted to be able to use his shower, so he placed salvaged galvanized sheet metal over the walls. He now calls it his "two-hour shower." The salvaged porcelain sink was picked up at a rebuilding center, closet dowels were used for the ceiling, rough-cut salvaged siding was used for the walls, leftover stone tile from a remodeling project was used on the floor, and a salvaged metal pipe functions as a curtain rod. This "temporary" bathroom has now become permanent—at least for the time-being.

▶ Look closely and you'll see that the wall is all metal cabinetry. The contrast between the wall of stainless-steel cabinets and the vintage door and knob adds to the beauty of this design. The marble sink is also a great design detail. Look for stainless-steel cabinets from commercial buildings or second-hand kitchen supply centers; vintage trough-like sinks can be found at your local architectural salvage shop.

▶▶ This commercial refrigerator was found at a recycle center and cost just a tenth of the original price (though the cost of running it is higher than that of an Energy Star-rated appliance). It was purchased before the home was designed and thus easily incorporated into the space. The school clock is also a vintage piece.

efficient. Even old gas appliances use a significant amount of gas to keep the pilot light running even when the appliance is not being operated. Unless you are really trying to minimize upfront cost or don't plan to use the appliance much, going with new or reproduction pieces that are Energy Star-rated is the best choice. Many of today's appliances are made with significant percentage of recycled metal.

STRUCTURAL ELEMENTS TO CONSIDER

Rust can be an issue when you're considering salvaged metal, so you should think about the end use of the material carefully. If the rust is simply on the surface, it can be wire-brushed off and the piece can be treated and painted (see the section on finishes, sealing and installation at the end of the chapter). However, if you are considering a metal grate for the entranceway, on which people will be stamping their feet, the metal needs to be as structurally sound as possible and rust-free.

If you're using a salvaged iron rack for hanging pots and pans, the metal should also be sound, and structural elements, such as additional bracing in the ceiling trusses, should be installed as necessary to adequately carry the weight. Old bathtubs should also be checked for structural integrity, especially near the tub feet and the plumbing fixtures.

Old pieces such as cast-iron tubs and sinks may have smaller plumbing fittings then are standard today. It is important to plan ahead and find fixtures with the correct fitting sizes, figure out where to have them modified, or have them special-ordered. In many older cast-iron tubs and sinks, pieces of the enamel may be missing; this can be repaired (professionally or with a

▲ This mudroom is a perfect example of repurposing an entire kitchen during a remodeling project. The old porcelain utility sink, cherry cabinetry, and older dishwasher were moved to the back entrance for the laundry and gardening rooms. The dishwasher isn't as energy-efficient as today's appliances, but it is rarely used and is a great backup.

▶ This mudroom incorporates a cast-iron sink with enamel coating that was purchased at architectural salvage shop. The sink comes in handy in this country home when the kids return from playing outside and the homeowner comes in from gardening. The homeowners sanded the metal base of the sink and painted it the same color as the walls. The vintage stained glass was a gift from their parents, which they put on an outside wall and added an energy panel to insulate it.

do-it-yourself kit found at a hardware store) or left as is to add to the character. Many homeowners repaint the outside of the tub to match the décor of the bathroom.

The durability of a metal counter or sink relates to the thickness of the metal. A smaller-gauge number is thicker than a larger-gauge number—for example, an 18-gauge sink is thinner and may be noisier and dent more easily than a heavier, 12-gauge sink.

CHALLENGES WITH METAL

Figuring out the type of metal something is made of is sometimes a guessing game. If you are not sure, ask the salvage professional. It may not matter to you what type of metal it is, but it is important to consider so that you know how to care for it properly. Each metal has its own care issues—copper patinas, aluminum planks can bow slightly if they are too light and not held down with adhesive, brass dulls and will need to be polished, older metal fixtures may have lead in them or the underlying piping may not be wide enough for today's standards. When using metal products that are heavy, having structurally sound support in the ceilings, floors, or walls should be considered during the design phase so that additional support can be placed before the piece is added. There are a variety of issues to consider when using metals, but they are all easily overcome with some detective work.

FINISHES, SEALING, AND INSTALLATION

Chips in the enamel covering on a cast-iron piece can add character, but if the chip is deep enough that the metal shows through, the metal may get compromised by water, causing it to rust and weaken. As mentioned earlier, repairing enamel can be done by a professional, but chip-repair kits from the hardware store are easy to use and cost less. Make sure the area is thoroughly clean and then sand the chip and the edges before following the directions on the kit. If the enamel is colored, follow the additive directions

Cast-iron tubs with enamel finishes are in abundance and give character to every type of bathroom. Modern, country, classic, or even cottage-style homes can incorporate a cast-iron tub. Many of these tubs have claw feet; others are built-in with full sides. This guest bathroom has a romantic feel with a simple white curtain over a cast-iron tub. The metal sides were painted a dark color and the claw feet were painted silver to blend with the octagon tile. The floor shows how much you can do with even small amounts of salvage material—the salvaged white tile pieces scattered across it are few in number but add a unique design element to the bathroom.

or contact the manufacturer of the sink to see if they have an exact-match color additive that they can send you.

Metal tiles come in a range of finishes. They can be rough, giving a more stone like look, or smooth (matte or polished) for a cleaner finish. The metal and the type of finish will determine whether or not it needs to be sealed. The backs of metal tiles are sand-blasted for a strong adhesion when using flooring adhesive or thin set. Make sure the thickness of the metal tile matches standard tile thickness; if it doesn't, additional material or thin set may be necessary to bring the tile floor up to match edging of other rooms. If you are using aluminum tiles, which are lightweight, weigh them down (for additional pressure) while the thinset or adhesive cures.

The type of metal and its location or placement will determine the installation methods. For example, installing metal tiles is similar to installing other types of tile, but because glossy metal tiles can scratch easily, it is helpful to mask the tile with tape before the grout is placed and the excess grout is washed off. If working with rusty metal, keep in mind the following: Getting cut without an updated tetanus shot can be dangerous, so plan ahead. Rusty metal also stains, so it should first be sealed if you plan to use it anywhere someone sits or walks.

This salvaged metal grate serves as a heating vent in the living room. There are many more throughout the home, some used for other purposes.

The living room fireplace of this dramatic coastal home pays homage to a breathtaking view of the ocean and the famous Haystack Rock, which can be seen through a wall of windows to the right of the fireplace. The boulders were salvaged from the property itself and from a friend who had just completed a landscaping project. This new home was built to be structurally prepared for the weight of the fireplace. The floors are salvaged Douglas fir and the beams are also from salvaged wood.

Stone, Concrete, Brick, and Ceramics

From boulders the size of small cars to fine grains of sand, stone is a natural material that may be a little more challenging to salvage, but it includes an extensive array of product choices, from natural stone, to brick, concrete, and ceramics. These salvaged variations are most commonly used in fireplace surrounds, countertops, and floors. Think of salvaged ceramic tiles framing a bathtub, an entryway floor made of vintage bricks, or a contemporary fireplace surround using salvaged stone aggregate concrete—all are creative designs accomplished by knowing the variety of materials available.

▸ The inset photo shows a "before" picture of a ranch-house fireplace that was off-center in the living room and a bit out of date.

The fireplace after renovation is a big improvement. The homeowner found real stone veneer on Craigslist and purchased the vintage wood board at an architectural salvage shop. Because it was a veneer, the homeowner was able to have the stonemason place the veneer right over the old brick without adding any additional structural support. This affordable salvage solution transformed the entire living room.

STONE

Stone seems like it's practically everywhere, so why bother searching for a salvaged version, you may wonder. The answer is that the kinds of stone most often used in interior design—granite, soapstone, slate, marble—are mined, not found on the surface of the land. Large swathes of land are destroyed in the energy-intensive mining process, upsetting animal habitats and other ecosystems. Exotic stone is not only mined but then shipped a great distance as well, adding to the energy output (and carbon footprint). Its weight only adds to the issue.

This is why it's better to search out stone companies in your area. Not only do you support the local economy this way, but you also reduce the energy output for travel. Plus, by staying close to home, you can see for yourself the environment your stone comes from. Of course, using salvaged stone is an even more eco-friendly choice. Many of these local stone companies carry salvaged products.

Types of Salvaged Stone

There are many types of salvaged stone—river rock, slate, soapstone, granite, marble, and more. Many homeowners choose to use stone in their home projects, incorporating it in its natural form or cutting it to create a veneer. Either way, most projects will have leftover material that can be reused in new projects, and even if you don't have quite enough leftover material for, say, your new fireplace surround or kitchen backsplash, you can usually find the last bit of matching stone at a stone company to finish the job.

MARBLES AND GRANITES Marble or granite countertops are common features of kitchens these days. Large pieces of salvaged marble or granite can be found and incorporated in your home design to look like a single, continuous slab. Another option is to collect smaller tiles from a few local locations until you have enough, or combine the small tiles with pieces of other sizes and types of stone used as accents. Creating a design around the materials you have will give you an interesting, unique look. Salvaged slabs can be installed as is with their rough edges or cut to match the other salvaged tile you may

SIBLEY
BIRDS

◀ The natural stone used for this fireplace is a mix of stone from a local stone company and leftover stone from a seawall the owners built on their property. The soapstone pieces on the floor in front of the fireplace were salvaged. During the remodeling project the homeowners kept the original metal firebox.

▶ Small pieces of salvaged marble in a variety of sizes are available in abundance and can be used to create unique patterns, as in this tiled bathroom. The antique sink, lights, mirrors, and fixtures add to its elegance.

have. Marble or granite aggregates, mixed with concrete and then highly polished, are also very popular as a flooring material. This type of salvaged material is usually seen in commercial buildings or hotels.

SLATE AND SOAPSTONE A popular look in kitchens and for flooring, reclaimed slate can come from a variety of places, from old school blackboards to slate roof shingles. Salvaged soapstone can be found in vintage laundry sinks and old counter pieces. Both of these types of stone are easy to work with and can be used effectively in any style of home design. Of course, one of the best ways to use salvaged slate roof tiles is to reuse them on a roof again. There is something very solid and grounded about a home that has a slate roof. It offers a feeling of permanence and character that is hard to match.

Salvaged slate from old roof tiles can be as large as 14 by 24 inches—as deep as a counter. Most tilework has a grout line, but slate that is cut to give a flat edge can be pushed together with a very thin—(almost invisible)—grout line using clear or black epoxy, giving the counter an almost continuous stone look. Slate roof shingles are thin, but you can make them look thicker on a counter by adding a small edge to the facing of the counter, creating a lip on the edge. Sometimes adhering a piece of reclaimed wood underneath will help to buttress the stone and give it a thicker, finished look.

Slate can range in color from green to black, depending on the type of slate and where it comes from. Most countertop-type slate comes from the New England area. Soapstone is

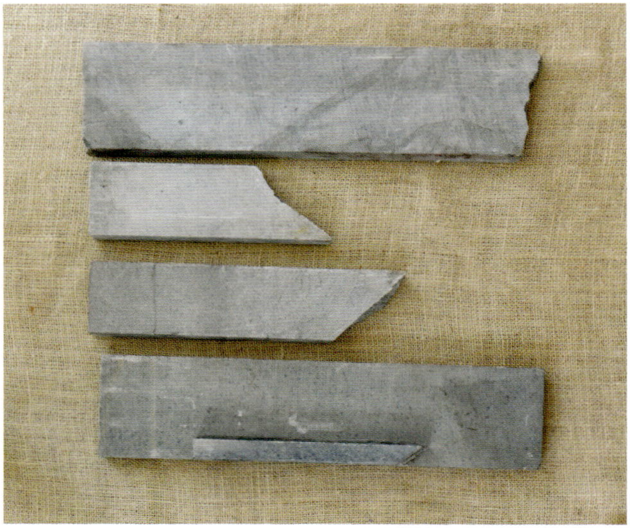

These pieces of soapstone, found in a discard pile at a stone center, were used to create backsplashes for a kitchen. With enough pieces and time, tile can be easily created from rough leftover pieces of stone such as these. One consideration is the thickness of the pieces; look for consistency in thickness so the tile will lie flat when installed. Soapstone is a soft stone and can be sanded easily in the case of unevenness.

The soapstone pieces in place after installation. The stone was cut to fit the backsplash size, black epoxy was used, and then after a slight sanding, it was mineral-oiled.

Using salvaged pieces of soapstone, the homeowners saved thousands of dollars and got the same clean look that full-piece counters provide.

Caffè Amaretto

An excellent example of the look you can achieve with just a few pieces of salvaged stone tile.

EVERY LITTLE BIT COUNTS!

Many homeowners have small piles of stone, tile, or similar material sitting in their basement or garage that they can't use but believe are too small to give to a recycle or salvage shop. Not so! If everyone contributed by bringing these excess materials to a local recycle center or salvage shop, a larger, more varied supply of salvaged goods would be available for homeowners to choose from, and the need for mining new stone would be reduced.

generally a grayish color but turns almost black when mineral oil is applied to it. The oil is used not only to give the stone that almost-black semi-gloss color but also to seal it, as soapstone is porous material and will stain without the sealer. Old laundry soapstone basins make for great, unique sinks, and soapstone pieces work well for counters and backsplashes because they are easy to cut. Soapstone has great minimalist look and feels like butter under your touch.

CULTURED STONE

For homeowners and designers who want the look of natural stone but need to save money, cultured stone is a good option. A mix of aggregates, dyes, and lightweight cement, it looks a lot like natural

▾ A bedroom can get cluttered with lots of things—bureaus, end tables, and everyday items. Large master closets help to store these needed items and keep the bedroom simple and uncluttered. This illustration shows a way to keep it not only simple but also fun. Salvaged pieces of chalkboard (or another similar material) with some built-in salvaged-wood shelving are just enough for a reading light and book and maybe a message or two.

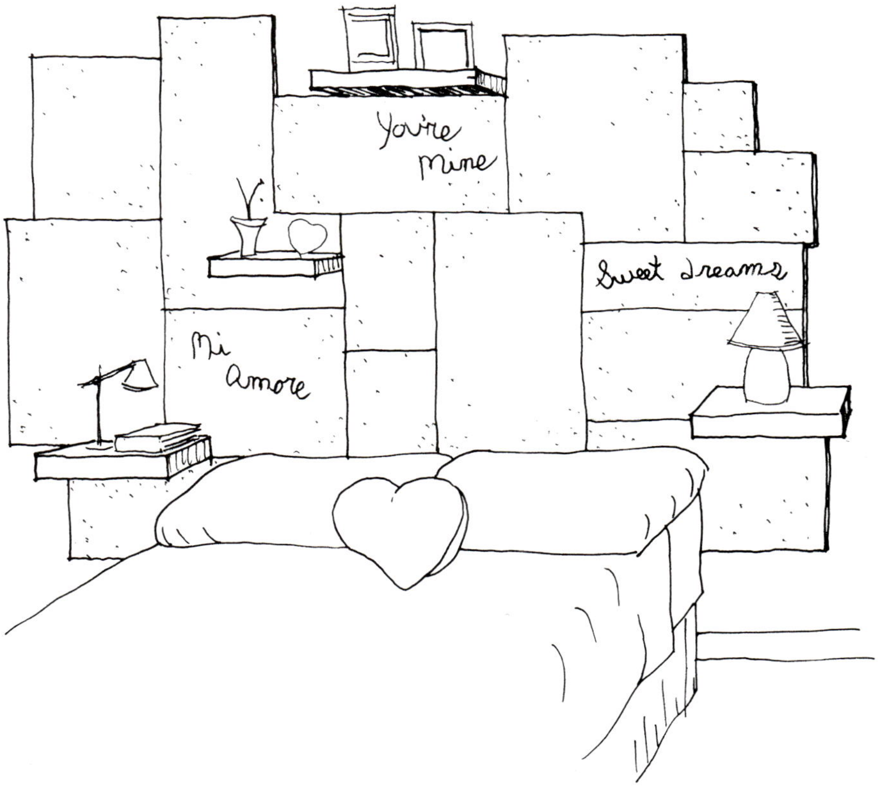

▲ A salvaged slate piece was used as the sink's base, with a drop-in sink. Salvaged tile and wainscoting finish off the design in this simple entranceway bath.

▶ The concrete brick fireplace in this living room makes a strong contemporary statement. Concrete, the world's most common manmade material, can now be manufactured with a large percentage of salvaged material, including fly ash and glass.

stone but is usually much less expensive, especially when used to face something like a fireplace or wall. (Real stone veneer is more expensive due to the labor involved in cutting it into thin slab.) Cultured stone can also be used for flooring, backsplashes, tub surroundings, and other interior locations where stone is used.

CONCRETE WITH SALVAGED AGGREGATE

Concrete, the most commonly used manmade material in the world, is a very multifaceted product. Composed of cement, water, and crushed stone, it is used for sidewalks, streets, foundations, buildings, roofing, and much more. In its traditional form, concrete is not usually considered a green product, due to the fact that it contains cement. The manufacturing of cement is extremely energy-intensive, requiring very high temperatures—up to 3,500 degrees Fahrenheit. In fact, it is thought that about 6% of the world's carbon-dioxide emission comes from the production of cement. Thankfully, more and more concrete mixtures used in home design are incorporating salvaged aggregates, such as glass terrazzo (see Chapter 2), stone aggregate, and fly ash (a by-product of coal-fired electric generating plants). These aggregates can replace most or all of the cement, making the production of concrete structures (counters, backsplashes, flooring, and so on) much more environmentally friendly. An additional benefit is that concrete with a salvaged aggregate can be poured on site to fit any size or dimension, from large slabs or blocks to smaller tiles.

Urbanite

Salvaged concrete roofing tiles, concrete blocks (cinderblocks), and old concrete laundry sinks can be repurposed

▲ Salvaged brick comes and goes quickly at recycle shops and salvage and rebuild warehouses. If you are looking for a large amount of salvaged or antique brick, you may want to call around and see if a shop can find it for you. Some companies specialize in restoration brick pieces. Don't forget to ask your local stone company or mason—many times they carry salvaged products as well.

▶ The mudroom of this home is filled with salvaged finds, including salvaged brick that a mason found for the homeowner. With a busy family and many animals, the brick floor allows for messy feet without too much trouble. (Brick is a porous material so if stains are an issue you will need to periodically seal the brick and the grout.) The salvaged soapstone sink helps with all sorts of gardening projects as well as with feeding the animals and washing up after a swim at the swimming hole. The front door, wall sconce, and faucet are antiques that were purchased at an architectural salvage shop.

and used in the exact same form without having to be crushed and recycled. But there is a lot of concrete out there—sidewalks, buildings, and roads—that can't be used as is. This type of concrete is called "urbanite." Due to its long life and sheer heft, urbanite is notoriously difficult—and expensive—to dispose of, and because of that it can be found in piles at landfills, town maintenance yards, and alongside roads. Although these large chunks can't be used for most interior design, they are great for fill, foundations of homes, or patio pieces. You can cut to size pieces reclaimed from the property site, or visit a local concrete recycle facility or salvage shop which may offer pieces that have been broken down by a portable crusher. Slowly, more and more towns are making concrete recycling available for those who want to make an effort in recycling their own pieces.

BRICK

Brick is composed of clay that is usually baked in a kiln. When considering brick, many people picture the traditional red, 8 x 2 inch form of it, but once you begin your search you will quickly realize that there are hundreds of varieties, colors, and textures available, in addition to different manufacturing processes and finishes. It is best to find all the brick you need from one source so you can ensure you are getting uniform brick for your project. Reclaimed brick from warehouses, old buildings, or even walkways can be used in a variety of ways in a home design. Pave an entire kitchen floor with bricks for a rustic feel, or use it for an entranceway floor, a fireplace, or a full wall for a distinctive look. Older reclaimed brick that is hand-built gives a feel similar to that of vintage wood, bringing character that is hard to find in newer products. Salvaged brick can also be easily cut to create a veneer for projects in locations that can't handle the weight or width of full brick, such as older homes or upper stories in modern homes.

CERAMICS AND PORCELAIN

Distinguishing between porcelain and regular ceramics can be very difficult. "True" porcelain contains only kaolin, flint, and feldspar, a mixture that is then fired at an extremely high temperature to create the white, translucent material we all picture when we think of porcelain. But the word porcelain is also used more generally to describe hundreds of different types, colors, shapes, and sizes of tiles and other products. One way to distinguish porcelain tiles from regular ceramic tiles is to look at the front and the back. Ceramic tiles usually have a glaze on the top and a red base.

This old porcelain surgeon sink is a great salvage find and works perfectly in the bathroom.

In addition to tile, doorknobs, sinks, tubs, and toilets are other common types of salvaged ceramic and porcelain products. Some may be enameled, which indicates a coating of porcelain over a metal. In general, you'll find that a true porcelain item is more expensive than a ceramic or enameled one.

Ceramic and porcelain tiles no longer usually used for kitchen countertops because of their uneven surface, grout lines that easily stain, and hardness, which can cause dishware to shatter with the slightest knock. But they still make great kitchen backsplashes or floor material (with darker grouts). Recycle centers and salvage shops always have piles of leftover ceramic and porcelain tiles from a variety of home projects. You can easily mix and match the tiles to achieve a checkerboard pattern for a bathroom, create a mosaic for a dramatic entranceway floor, or even hand-paint the tiles (and seal them with epoxy) to give your room a Portuguese or Italian style. Salvaged ceramic and porcelain tiles are very affordable and can easily be installed by a handy homeowner.

DESIGN TIP

Most people would think twice about reusing an old toilet—personal hygiene issues and water-flow efficiency (an old toilet can waste up to 4,000 gallons of water a year) are just two of the reasons why. But don't throw that old toilet in the dumpster! Recycling programs across the nation crush old porcelain toilets into small pieces for use in roads, foundations, and drainage. They can even be used in interior home design as the salvaged aggregate in concrete for countertops and flooring. That will make quite a conversation piece in your home! (The metal in the toilets is recycled and melted down for other products.) Contact the solid-waste district in your hometown to see how you can get some crushed toilet pieces for your own salvage projects.

▲ This handful of tile was pulled from a pile at a salvage shop, sanded slightly, hand-painted, and then covered with a sealer. (You have to seal hand-painted tiles or the paint will wash off with water.) Painted tiles can be used for a backsplash, trim for the bathroom, or even as an entire wall system in any space that does not get a lot of use or wear. Note that the sealed tile is too slippery for flooring.

◄ You can find piles and piles of salvaged ceramic and porcelain tile pieces at recycle and architectural shops. Whites, blues, and pinks are just a few of the colors available. Look through these piles before you head out to buy new tile—you will be surprised at what you can find. Remember to always look at the tile in natural light to accurately match the colors, even white tiles.

Make the most of affordable salvaged tiles: the tiles could be hand-painted in a blue Mediterranean pattern and installed both on the wall and around the drop-in salvaged acrylic tub. Use dimensional lumber painted white for flooring and a salvaged piece of wood for the shelf. Add a line of the crystal light globes you usually see on ceilings, put them on a dimmer, and you have just created a romantic bathroom.

If you want to use a new product that matches your design plan, you can now buy ceramic tiles that are made out of salvaged light bulbs, glass, and recycled porcelain. They use a low-VOC (volatile organic compound) adhesive and are biodegradable. This is sometimes a great option for homeowners who need a large amount, specific color, or certain style of tile.

POSSIBLE USES

Salvaged stone, brick, concrete, or ceramic can all go a long way in adding character to any design you may want to achieve. You can certainly use more than one of these materials, but keep in mind that you want the overall look to be consistent and flow visually. Using brick for floors and concrete for your countertop is a fairly heavy look, but the two materials can work well together if the rest of the room design accommodates it. Whatever the stone or stone-like product you select, make sure to strike the right balance in the space and use products that complement each other. Color, size, and shape, are all factors in creating a design that incorporates stone in a smart, eye-catching way.

Fireplaces

Salvaged brick, natural stone, slate roof tiles, slabs of marble, and even poured concrete with salvaged aggregate can all be used to create a fireplace surround. If you're going for a modern, minimalist look, consider large chunks of salvaged urbanite or pieces of granite, marble or slate in their natural state and place them around in a simple gas fireplace.

Sinks

Antique marble sinks, white porcelain farmhouse sinks and vintage soapstone, slate, or concrete laundry sinks are just a few of the favorites among homeowners looking for character in their washrooms or kitchens. All of these items can be readily found, and although they may cost more than simple stainless steel, the character they add will more than make up for their cost. Many soapstone, slate and concrete sinks come in a deep,

This vintage slate surround was found at an antique store. The antique mirror and detailed surround provide a strong aesthetic for the woodstove, which serves as the central heat source in the master bedroom on cold winter nights. The flooring is made from salvaged wood as well.

This home features many salvaged items. The top of the half wall is capped with salvaged lumber. The vintage marble sink sits on an old pine cupboard, and the shelving is reclaimed wood that was rough cut, lightly sanded, and oiled.

single- or double-bowl style. Originally used in basements as laundry sinks, some still have their original metal or wood base.

Roofs

Salvaged slate roofing shingles (or tiles) can be placed back on roofs. When searching them out look for ones that are uniformly thick. Weather causes the surface of the shingles to spall off, leaving the shingle thinner. Eventually, ice, water, and wind will cause the thinner shingles to crack and break. (Remember

Reclaimed slate roof from an old building really makes a statement on this new home. A salvaged slate roof is more costly than a new asphalt roof, but it gives even a new home the look and feel of an old country estate. Slate, a natural stone, will also last longer and is more eco-friendly than a manmade asphalt roof, which will need replacing down the road. If you are thinking about using salvaged slate, plan ahead and look into its costs and installation requirements, including weight considerations.

◂ The countertops in this lakeside, cottage-style home were made from slate chalkboard salvaged from an old school. The homeowner sanded away thirty years' worth of chalk dust and then edged the slate with a piece of wood (painted a matching black) to make it look thicker. This was a very affordable solution for their budget.

▸ On this wall, different salvaged pieces of stone and tile, placed to create a geometric pattern, are not only are visually pleasing but also shield the wall from the heat of the salvaged woodstove.

that the upper portion of each shingle will be under the shingles above it and therefore not subject to erosion.) Don't pick shingles that are broken around the nail holes.

Alternatives to slate are salvaged concrete or clay roofing tiles, found in abundance in southern homes. These may be easier to find at a local recycle center or through companies that specialize in vintage roofing tiles.

Counters

Salvaged soapstone pieces cut into tiles, recycled blackboard slate, and poured concrete with glass or fly ash aggregate are just a few ways to use salvaged stone for a countertop. All of these are good choices for counters because they can be sanded and polished for a smooth surface—the smoother the surface, the easier it will be to clean and maintain.

Walls

A thin veneer of brick or stone can add character to the walls of any room without requiring the extra space needed when the material is used in its whole form. In a kitchen, a brick or stone wall with built-in shelves can add warmth and depth.

Flooring

As suggested earlier, large, flat pieces of salvaged slate can be used for an entranceway or in a sunroom. A brick floor in a country home or cabin can be provide a rustic look; salvaged concrete made with recycled aggregate, such as stone chips, recycled glass, or fly ash, can give a sleek, modern look.

The floor of this master bedroom is concrete, giving a simple, clean look. Salvaged aggregate in concrete can be powder-fine for a smooth texture or larger (pebble-sized) for one that's more mottled. The ceiling is proof that pieces of salvaged plywood can add depth and warmth to a space as well as offer an affordable alternative to other ceiling-material options. Outside, the garage door salvaged from an industrial building, placed on barn-door trackers, creates a visual focal point in the courtyard and allows easy access to a workshop. The unique wall of salvaged wood was mentioned in the wood chapter, on page 37. The opposite wall (at right) are slates of salvaged decking board.

This bedroom fireplace is a cozy place to curl up next to and read a good book. The home was designed to accommodate the weight of the salvaged brick as well as the modern, energy-efficient gas fire. The homeowner used the salvaged brick itself as the mantel, adding some depth without disrupting the flow of the structure from floor to ceiling.

STRUCTURAL ELEMENTS TO CONSIDER

First and foremost, if you are thinking about using salvaged stone in an interior project, weight is a primary factor that must be considered as the structural design concepts are worked on. When building a new home, the structural considerations can be addressed well in advance, before work has begun. However, in a renovation or remodeling project, it is best to consult an expert (an architect or

structural engineer) to be sure the placement of the stone is appropriate for the location. For example, if you want a brick accent wall, you need to be certain beforehand that the wall system in place can withstand the weight of the material. A brick or stone veneer can be a good choice if structural problems arise. Also, some older bricks are not as structurally sound as newer salvaged bricks and cannot be used for a load-bearing wall or surface. Understand the structural integrity of your salvaged stone and you can place it properly.

CHALLENGES WITH STONE, CONCRETE, BRICK, AND CERAMICS

It is important not to store pieces of marble, or granite, or other stone flat—they need to be propped upright until they are laid down for installation. They can easily break if not handled properly. Cutting up pieces of salvaged stone needs to be done with a steady hand, especially if cutting into tiles to create numerous tiles of the same size and butting the tiles up to one another with no grout line. If you do use a grout line, there is some forgiveness in the layout. When it comes to working with ceramics, especially glazed ceramic tiles, be sure to use a tile cutter made specifically for ceramics to avoid chipping the edges of the glaze.

Be careful when considering salvaged porous stones, such as concrete slabs from industrial facilities. They may have absorbed toxins due to spills of oil or other substances.

◀ The dark soapstone sink in this country kitchen offers a beautiful contrast to the warm walls and salvaged trim. The old school light works as soft task lighting and adds to the charm.

◀◀ When looking for salvaged stone pieces at an architectural or rebuilding shop, ask someone for help. The slabs of stone are usually standing up on their ends and sometimes are pushed between wood frames to keep them from moving, which makes them difficult to see. Also, the pieces can be very heavy and it is better to have the owner of the shop move them around so you can see each of them.

▲ Lined up in an architectural salvage shop, these basins are ready for their new home. Many will already have their hardware and stands. Find a matching pair and create a unique master bathroom.

▶ This guest bathroom shows a wonderful example of a salvaged marble top that came with the vanity and the faucets and hardware. The homeowner had only to put the plumbing in place. More salvaged touches can be found in the glass door, vintage wall sconces, and medicine cabinet.

Weight is always something that is underestimated. A river rock fireplace surround may not look terribly large, but when you consider the weight of the firebox itself, the number of boulders needed, and then the grout, you begin to realize that the pounds add up. As mentioned earlier remodeling projects may need to incorporate additional structural support, or stone veneers can be considered. New homes should be designed with the structural needs considered at the outset. Stone is not an "afterthought" type of salvaged material!

If not sealed properly, porous materials—such as soapstone, slate, bricks, and concrete—can stain. The type of stone or brick will determine the kind of sealer you need and how often to apply it.

Salvaged stone sinks may not be watertight and need to be pulled apart and re-epoxy (or glued) at the seams. Many stone suppliers will do this for a fee and some even sell rebuilt vintage and newer salvaged sinks.

FINISHES, SEALING, AND INSTALLATION

The type of finish you need will depend on whether salvaged stone is from raw material or something that has already been sealed. Porous stone and concrete products need to be sealed. The intended use will also affect the seal you choose—a countertop, for example, which will come into contact with food, will require a seal different from that of a floor.

A salvaged brick floor will need a brick masonry sealer; it is important that you thoroughly clean and dry the brick before applying the sealant. Older salvaged brick tends to be softer and can be damaged by a rough cleaning, so be sure to test a brick first. Once you have done the initial sealing of the brick floor, it will need an annual sealing after that. Brick walls and fireplaces surrounds can be sealed with a tung-oil-type sealer and then just cleaned with a vacuum or a little soap and water on a regular basis.

Soapstone must be sealed with mineral oil; when it starts to lose its shine in places, its time for a new application. Reapplication of the mineral oil will be needed more frequently at first (about every few months) because the stone is dry and will continue to suck up oil until it becomes more saturated.

Some types of slate need to be sealed

and others don't. Darker slate tends to be more porous and could use a sealer, something as simple as mineral oil. Some slates are used in exterior projects, such as walkways and patios, because they have a tendency to chip. When you find salvaged slate, make sure you learn about its properties so you can make the right design decisions.

If using salvaged slate shingles for a roof, you will need to use copper or stainless-steel nails, because other types of metal will not last as long as the shingle itself and will leave rust marks on the stone. Remember to look up the nailing process for salvaged slate shingles; they need to be nailed loosely to allow for expansion and contraction. And be sure to assess whether the roof is able to handle the weight of the material.

Marble and granite generally already have a polish on them, but often natural stone pieces will need a finish or sealant.

If a stone is used in a sink or tub, take an extra care with the finish to avoid water stains. A clear epoxy around the edges of the sink, where it meets the stone, can help keep water from leaking onto the stone.

Installation of stone will depend on its location and type. If it is a tile, a regular tile grout will work. Soapstone or slate countertops can use an epoxy, and brick, concrete, and natural stone can be put together by a mason with grout. The variety of grouts and epoxies available today is amazing, providing you with a range of colors and textures to choose from. Some are more moisture and mold-resistant than others, making them a great choice for bathrooms. As mentioned earlier, a black epoxy can be used with soapstone pieces pushed together to give a counter a continuous, solid look. Black or gray grout can also work well with salvaged tiles in a heavily-trafficked area, like a bathroom or entranceway. Installation of hand-painted tiles can transform a boring bathroom into a stunning Mediterranean retreat; unique stone pieces grouted together can turn a modern gas fireplace into a stunning piece of art. The possibilities are as endless as the salvaged pieces of stone themselves.

▲ This open cathedral-ceiling kitchen features examples of salvaged beams, flooring, and the beautifully balanced look of the two pieces of salvaged stone that flank the stove.

◀ Check the newspaper or local online message boards to find out about leftover stone from a neighbor's project.

◂ The lighting and cabinet hardware in this dining room and sitting area were made from salvaged aluminum. These custom-made pieces show that a striking modern room can incorporate salvaged pieces.

Lighting

When designing a home, you can never underestimate the importance of its orientation to the sun, the amount of natural light it gets, and the lighting components you will need. Consciously or subconsciously, people always notice the power of light. Warm sunlight streaming in through the windows offers a sense of peace, and lighting created to achieve a certain ambience makes a difference in how you feel in the space.

▸ The pendant lights over this island were once part of one light fixture. The art deco piece was recreated into three pendant task lights.

▸▸ Fun, unusual, eye-catching light fixtures can be great additions in certain areas of the home. Over dining-room tables, at the sides of a fireplace, in entranceways and stairways—these are just a few of the spots where lighting can enhance the design. This unique vintage light, purchased at a vintage lighting shop and then rewired, gives charm to the elegantly simple staircase. It gives a warm, calming glow as you climb the stairs to the private area of the house.

The great thing about lighting is that it is one of the most common salvaged items available today: Almost every antique shop, recycle shop, and architectural warehouse (not to mention specialty lighting shops) has an abundance of reclaimed, vintage, and antique lighting. The only hard part is figuring out which will look best with your design. Brass chandeliers, wall sconces, old schoolhouse pendants, art deco pieces, mid-century swag lamps—the choices are almost endless. You can even get creative and make your own fixture out of salvaged material.

There are a few home locations where interesting lighting can serve as the main design feature, allowing for a simpler design in the overall space. For example, a dining room with simple wall and window structures can be made stunning with the addition of the right chandelier. Lighting can be whimsical, elegant, modern, eclectic—each fixture creates its own sense of style and mood.

The other wonderful thing about salvaged lighting fixtures is that, unlike most older salvaged appliances, they can usually be rewired to comply with today's energy-efficient standards. Some don't even need rewiring—making them energy-efficient is as simple as changing the bulb. Incandescent light bulbs—what most of our homes today have—will soon be extinct.

This vintage sunburst-style art deco chandelier along with the wall sconces compliments the salvaged table and antique sideboard, creating a picture-perfect dining space in which to watch sunsets over the lake outside.

In 2012, a federal ban on 100-watt incandescent bulbs will go into effect, and by 2014 the 60-watt and 40-watt versions will also be gone from stores. Why? To improve energy efficiency. Approximately one-fourth of all home electricity use comes from lighting fixtures; switching to non-incandescent bulbs can save anywhere from 75 to 80% in energy consumption. Multiply that by the 110 million households in the U.S. (with an average of 50 to 100 light sockets per home), and you can see that the energy saving will be immense. Today's energy-efficient bulb choices are changing and expanding at—well, the speed of light. Compact fluorescent lights (CFLs) and light emitting diodes (LEDs) once came in limited sizes and shapes but now are available for almost every light fixture, salvaged or new.

TYPES OF SALVAGED LIGHT FIXTURES

Usually the older the fixture is, the more expensive it will be. Some, such as gaslight fixtures or iconic items like Stickley and Tiffany lamps, have become highly sought-after collectibles. These items usually come with hefty pricetags, but you get a valuable piece of art that will continue to hold that value for future generations. If you do choose to purchase a fixture that is advertised as a rare piece, have a lighting expert look at it before you lay down a chunk of cash. If you like the look of antique lighting but can't afford an original piece, there are many amazing reproductions—usually either wall sconces or chandeliers—that look almost exactly like the originals.

Ceiling Fixtures

An abundance of ceiling fixtures and glass shades from the 1950s, 60s, and 70s can be found at recycle shops. Installed anywhere from entranceways to closets and pantries, these affordable ceiling fixtures give a lovely character

Scanning the paper, the owner of this home found the piano pictured here at an auction for an affordable price. A vintage light fixture hangs above it and is functional as well as artistic. Found in a vintage lighting shop and subsequently rewired, the light glows when it is turned on giving the room a striking elegance and serving as a spotlight for the kids while they practice.

to any space. They can be installed flush to the ceiling or hung as pendants, which are wonderful above sinks, islands, or special spots in a room.

Chandeliers

There has been a resurgence of the use of chandeliers, especially ones with crystals and lots of glass. Extremely fancy vintage chandeliers can range in the thousands of dollars, or you can get creative and find a salvaged brass chandelier at a recycle center and remake it into your own fancy chandelier. With a little paint, some crystal teardrops, and even some decorative fabrics, you can fashion a unique chandelier for any room in the house.

Most chandeliers at recycle and antique shops don't have a plug, making it difficult to test if the wiring is good and if the fixture works. However, you can easily attach a plug, to the ends of the wire to test the light. Sometimes the shop will have one you can use, or you can pick one up at a nearby hardware store.

Wall Fixtures

Salvaged wall fixtures and sconces are usually used in bathrooms, sitting areas, and kitchens, often flanking a mirror or fireplace. The selection ranges from the 1970s Hollywood-style round-bulb light strips (usually used in bathrooms) to fixtures that look like old candle holders (great in dining rooms above a sideboard). Light fixtures custom made from recycled materials can make a windowseat or reading nook even more appealing. When designing the rooms, make sure the ceiling fixtures provide efficient lighting in the key locations; the wall fixtures can be used for smaller pools of light that add to the overall ambience.

▲ The immense variety of salvaged wall sconces makes them a highly versatile design element. They can be used in a range of places—in a bathroom framing a mirror, above a mantel or a painting, or in a dining room near a sideboard. In more and more homes, interesting wall sconces are now being used in place of bedside lamps.

◄ This salvaged chandelier gives the guest bathroom a romantic flair. The tub surround is concrete with salvaged glass and the bead board is made from repurposed trim from the owner's previous home.

▲ This light fixture made with recycled metal has a modern Asian flair. Outfitted with an energy-efficient bulb, the lights would be beautiful for an interior or exterior design.

▶ This is truly taking your recycling seriously! These bottles were found during the deconstruction phase of an old, condemned building on the property. The homeowner cut the bottoms off the bottles, threaded the wiring through the necks, and suspended them from an old window shutter. Tucked into a window seat, this dining room with its glowing light, is a great place not only for a meal but also just to hang out.

Homemade Light Fixtures

Salvaged barbwire, mason jars, electrical wire caps, industrial fixtures, and even beer bottles have been used to create lighting. Light fixture hardware can be found at your local hardware store and used for a do-it-yourself lighting project. If you are not comfortable working with electrical components but want a light fixture made out of a salvaged piece, take the components to your local lighting specialist and ask them to create a fixture for you. There are also a number of artisans and specialty lighting shops that are creative with vintage or unique objects, fabricating lighting with everything from paint cans and old glass insulators to pasta strainers and discarded computer hard drives. Whether you make it yourself or buy it already fabricated, a one-of-a-kind salvaged light fixture not only creates a unique style for your room but also will be a conversation piece for all your guests.

▲ This illustration shows an old wooden door with glass inset suspended from a ceiling with salvaged metal piping. (Make sure you consider structural issues with a heavy piece like this.) Place old holiday lights on top of the glass and string a wire up one of the pipes. These beautiful bulbs will shine through the glass onto your dining room table.

▶ A specialty lighting and metal workshop spends a great deal of time reconditioning antique lighting fixtures as well as creating new ones from unique salvage material.

CHALLENGES WITH SALVAGED LIGHTING

One of the challenges of using salvaged lighting fixtures is knowing whether or not an old fixture needs to be rewired. (Any fixture that has a cloth-covered wire needs to be rewired—that's an easy one. Others may be harder to access.) The thought of having to rewire an older fixture sometimes deter homeowners from considering salvaged or antique fixtures. But rewiring is not as difficult as most people assume, and if you really feel uncomfortable doing it yourself, you can always ask a lighting expert to rewire it for you; the size, complexity, and age of the fixture will determine the pricing. Otherwise, you can purchase a do-it-yourself kit from a hardware store or follow directions on a reputable home-repair website.

baking

DESIGN TIP

When choosing between compact fluorescent lights and LED lights, do some research because the bulb choices and efficiencies are changing rapidly. Plus, each type of bulb gives off a different color, warming or cooling a room, and some can be put on dimmers whereas others cannot. Understand the type of lighting you want to create in a room and then find the bulb that best matches it. Ambiance lighting, for example, will require a very different bulb than task lighting.

◂◂ The cooking area in this kitchen uses a salvaged light fixture for task lighting over the counter. The proportion of the light works perfectly with the space and the window. The hardware on the cabinets was salvaged from a farm building in the same town.

◂ Learning about lighting options is as much about the bulbs as the fixtures themselves.

▲ The "before" and "after" of a metal fixture can be dramatic depending on the age of the item, the oxidation, how it patinas, and how it was cleaned. Many homeowners prefer the look of aged brass; others like it clean and shiny.

▶ This is just a small sampling of the types of metals, finishes, and colors available in fixtures. Knowing the look and type of metal you like will make it easier for you to find the salvaged or vintage fixture that fits your design.

Another challenge is making sure your salvaged fixtures will work with energy-efficient bulbs. Double-check that the fixture you choose can be changed to meet the 2012 federal lighting changes or can be repurposed to handle more efficient bulbs.

Finding the right fixture for your room may take some time. The style and period of the home are two factors to think about; the size and scale of the space are also important considerations. A small, finely detailed chandelier, for example, may get swallowed up in a larger foyer; a 1950s pendant globe light might overwhelm a small guest-bedroom space.

FINISHES, SEALING, AND INSTALLATION

The way a fixture is finished will depend on the material it is made of and the look you want to achieve. Vintage copper and other metals may be best left alone, needing only a gentle cleaning before installation. The dark brown patina of brass may be perfect for a fixture in a den or study; a shiny, polished look may work better in the kitchen or bathroom.

If you are using a wood fixture that has old paint, you should consider sealing it with a technique or sealer mentioned in Chapter 1. Glass fixtures do not need finishing or sealing but always benefit from a gentle cleaning. Make sure to look for cracks or chips in glass fixtures. Many times they can be left alone but if the crack is significant you may want to consider getting another glass shade or light fixture.

Installation can be as simple as plugging in your salvaged fixture or as complicated as creating a specialized ceiling box stabilized between two joists to carry the weight of a heavy piece. Most lighting fixtures use a standard electrical outlet box but others will need additional mounting bracket pieces depending on the size and weight. Ceiling fixtures like chandeliers use a different mounting bracket than long florescent lights or wall-mounted lights. There are numerous websites that will guide you through the installation of the mounting brackets as well as the wiring process. If you don't feel completely competent in what you are doing, it is best to hire a professional. There are many lighting and electrical-outlet codes; following them isn't just about passing a housing inspection—it is a matter of safety.

A vintage table and mirror turned into a bathroom vanity with a copper candy-bowl sink make this an interesting, eclectic bathroom for guests. Vintage wall sconces warm up the space with soft lighting.

◂ This contemporary fireplace uses two salvaged granite steps as the hearth and a very old piece of Chinese wood as the mantel. Brought together with a simple concrete-and-brick surround, the fireplace achieves a great deal of character with just a couple of salvaged items. The floor is vintage reclaimed wood and the doors on either side of the fireplace that lead to the family room are also vintage. Together, they create a calming, modern look for this lakefront home.

Salvage

Why We Use It and Where to Find It

At this point it should be clear that using salvage is a good decision both financially and environmentally. But there are many other reasons to choose salvaged materials as well: It encourages us to respect our history, it creates jobs, it allows us to embrace wabi sabi (the Japanese art of finding beauty in imperfection), and teaches our children the importance of using materials we already have—a philosophy that can be passed down through generations to come.

Mike O'Brien, Green Building Specialist

Many homeowners, professionals, and artisans are dedicated to using salvaged material. In this chapter we talk to six well-respected professionals who tell us in their own words about their passion for salvage and why they encourage others to use it as well.

MIKE O'BRIEN

Green Building Specialist, Portland Bureau of Planning and Sustainability

My philosophy of reuse is to encourage people to think about intrinsic values rather than just looks, to know the story of where their house came from (and where it will go someday), and to be aware of their footprint. Without being mindful, efforts to have glossy new kitchens and interiors can bring toxics, slave labor, and ruined forests as a hidden dimension. When people visit our home and see for themselves what reused materials look like, I hope they will rethink their assumptions. For example, one assumption people make is that the building industry does not want to use salvaged material—but what I have learned is that the number one reason they rarely use it is because their clients don't ask. Well, we have an opportunity to change that. Let's all begin to ask and make a change for the better.

BRENDAN O'REILLY

Owner, Gristmill Builders

As a builder I have the unique opportunity to work with clients who already see the value of using salvaged material in their homes, but I also have the responsibility to be part of the change in the building industry and to encourage clients to see the beauty and spirit of adding materials from the past into their homes. To me, salvaged material is living art, and only when we are open to seeing all the possibilities it has to offer will we see—as an industry and as homeowners—the attraction of the past being a part of our lives today. When we use salvaged materials from old farms, an energy comes from the material—all those years of protecting the animals, the love of the work and the grounding earth, are still in it and can be felt when it's placed lovingly into a new home. Clients often ask for the salvaged material, and I hope that—through exceptional designs and builders who love to work with the material—all builders will begin to embrace the unique style of salvaged material.

Brendan O'Reilly, Owner, Gristmill Builders

DAVID KNOX

Owner, Mason Brothers Architectural Salvage

Architectural salvage warehouses are usually overflowing with pedestal sinks, fireplace mantels, stained-glass windows, reclaimed flooring and timbers, lighting and furnishings, as well as hundreds of doors—both old and new, stripped and original-finish. The clients are homeowners and contractors—some renovating older homes, others using older materials in new construction. The old adage "they don't make things like they used to" is evident at an architectural salvage shop. As more and more building professionals and homeowners become concerned about

David Knox, Owner, Mason Brothers Architectural Salvage

disappearing heritage and to avoid unhealthful building materials, there is a growing awareness that older is, indeed, better.

Architectural salvage centers tend to have a large selection of unique and affordable materials, including wood, glass, windows, doors, hardware, and fixtures. Most building-material centers receive their inventory from deconstructed houses and buildings, which can bring in a wealth of unique, one-of-a-kind pieces that can be turned into very special and functional items. By making something new from something old, you can feel good about the positive impact you have on the world by keeping some previously used building materials out of the landfill. You use less new raw material and you help your own community by supporting small-business owners and their employees.

SHANNON QUIMBY

REX Project Homeowner, Salvage Designer, Author, and Television Host

It's a common sight in most neighborhoods: dumpster after dumpster parked near home-construction jobs full of material that's destined for the landfill. When we broke ground on our new home, the REX Project (Reuse Everything Experiment), I vowed no dumpster would be seen on site, let alone used. In less then seven months we deconstructed the existing house (it was falling down) and infused 99% of it into our new home built at the same location. And I am not just talking about the easy stuff like

Shannon Quimby, REX Project Founder, Salvage Designer, Author, and Television Host. Photo by Steve Cridland.

all the wood products—framing, flooring, doors, and cabinetry. We took it ten steps further and reused the concrete, insulators, stinky carpet, and even the sink drain. Fixtures were salvaged; windows became mirrors; even the nails were saved as decorative art. The flashing, water heaters, air conditioner—all our metal scraps were melted down and supported our recycled metal roof. But everyone's favorite is the dining-room chandelier, which we made from vintage wine bottles we found in the former garden hedge. We succeeded and found a place for everything. And it made me realize that average homeowners, like me, can make a huge difference in the building industry by setting the example that if I can do this, anyone can.

It's my mission to do away with dumpsters. Let's show the next generation that this type of home construction is the norm. This is how we do it—we don't even think about it—it's a part of our lives.

Shane Endicott, Executive Director, the ReBuilding Center

SHANE ENDICOTT

Executive Director, the ReBuilding Center

I believe the ability to reuse salvaged materials that we carry out with our community-run nonprofit organization is just one piece of a bigger story. Through waste diversion, we can support our local community with affordable resources, create jobs, teach valuable building skills, preserve natural resources, and inspire everyone to work together. Starting with deconstruction services—an affordable and sustainable alternative to conventional demolition, with a skilled crew—we are able to help homeowners and commercial-building owners salvage up to 85% of their building. Turning a liability (the salvaged material that might end up in a landfill) into an asset puts money in the community and gives homeowners affordable alternatives to building. This is just the beginning of strengthening the social fabric we call our community.

TIM FROST

Chairperson, Green Council of Vermont Homebuilders and Remodelers, and Owner, Peregrine Design/Build

As the chairperson for the Green Council for our regional building association I am excited to learn more about the best practices when it comes to green building. It is imperative that we educate not only our industry professionals but also the homeowners we work for. Working together, the building trades are able to change how we build for the next generation. One of the focuses of the Green Council is using reclaimed materials and reducing the amount of materials that end up at our landfills, which is one of the industry's biggest concerns. A big opportunity for reusable materials comes from the older housing stock, where you have timbers, flooring, and architectural components that can be reused. When incorporating these pieces into a new design you can add stunning beauty and character while helping to "green" our building practices.

WHERE TO FIND IT

Many people get nervous about entering an architectural shop or recycle center. They are overwhelmed—but this is where the fun part begins. Walk around to get a feel for what the store has to offer and go from section to section and look at the pieces. Ask yourself: Can I use these lights in my home? Does this tub fit in the guest bathroom? Should I use vintage drawer pulls? What can I do with these pieces of ceramic tile? Can I be creative with these wood cabinets? The possibilities are endless—all you have to do is look at the salvaged piece or material and see how it can be what you want it to be. Remember to look beyond the dirt or small repairs—an "ugly duckling" piece of wood or grimy light fixtures can be turn into a swan with a little sanding or polishing. Embrace the piles and cull out the special pieces that will make your home design shine. If that still seems overwhelming, bring a list of needed items and a friend who is passionate about salvage and whose ideas you respect, and they'll help put you on the right path.

Once homeowners have overcome any preconceived notions, stigmas, or fears, they find they enjoy the "treasure hunting" part of the salvage-design process. And once they start to do the research themselves—even if they are working with designers and builders—they may find themselves becoming addicted. Another reason it is great for homeowners to embrace this part of the search is to help keep the costs in check. It is some-

Tim Frost, Chairperson, Green Council of Vermont Homebuilders and Remodelers, and Owner, Peregrine Design/Build

Looking for door knobs? Would you like glass, metal, wooden, or porcelain? Salvaged material is in abundance—all you have to do is take the time to look for it.

Plan ahead for larger pieces such as sinks, doors, and appliances to ensure that your design incorporates these elements without incurring additional costs for changes after construction has begun.

times difficult for a builder, designer, or architect to encourage the use of salvaged material because it can be costly and they don't want to pass that cost on to their client—who may not always understand why something costs so much. And unless builders have their own salvaged materials, already know where to find them, or are working with a homeowner who has already selected salvaged pieces, it can become a time-consuming search.

If you are just beginning your home building or remodeling project, it will take a little bit of research and a handful of contacts to collect your own circle of salvage experts who will have (or be able to find) everything you need for

Use an old store counter as cabinetry or as a freestanding island; a metal gate can work as a pot rack or even a fireplace screen. These are just a few of the ideas you can come up with when you walk into a salvage shop and start to look around. It's like a treasure hunt!

your project. Whether you rely on someone else to find your salvaged pieces or you do it yourself, there are a few tried-and-true places to search.

Architectural Salvage Shops

These types of shops will be very important during your search because many of their products have architectural significance. Vintage lighting, cast-iron or porcelain sinks, antique or vintage wood for flooring, pieces of marble tops, beams for ceilings, countertops, and large cabinetry pieces for islands or vanities—the list goes on and on. Visiting these shops in person will give you a feeling of the history of the pieces, but many of these shops have items on websites as well, which is convenient and can save time. Owners or employees of these shops may also be able to help you search a particular piece out. If you are planning a large project that will incorporate a number of salvaged pieces, it's a good idea to get to know the folks at your local architectural

Something as simple as a vintage light fixture and some salvaged wood can contribute a lot to a space in your home. Even if you just do a little bit at a time, it will make a huge difference in the long run.

▲ Look outside the box. This homeowner purchased an antique cabinet to use in place of a built-in closet in their guest bedroom. They not only used salvaged materials but also saved labor and material costs this way. Plus, the cabinetry adds a lot of character to the small space.

▸ At recycle centers you will find more modern tubs—even Jacuzzi tubs—and other modern fixtures.

salvage shop. They are experts at what they do and they can advise you on particular pieces and how to care for them.

Many of these shops also carry practical items that may not have historic value but will fit your salvage needs, such as glass doors for showers or tempered glass windows so remember to think of them when you are looking for basic salvaged materials as well.

Antique Shops

Movable cabinetry, lighting fixtures, hardware—smaller salvaged items such as these are what you will usually find in antique shops. They are also a great place to find vanities for bathrooms, large farmhouse tables that can be used instead of a built-in island, or even pie cupboards or large storage cabinets to use in place of closets or pantries.

Recycle Shops and Rebuild Centers

Recycle shops and rebuild centers carry a wide range of items, including metal, glass, and wood doors; single- and double-paned windows; glass block, brick, and stone; dimensional lumber and trim pieces; shutters; ceramic tiles; everyday brass fixtures; hardware; sinks, toilets, and shower stalls; and cabinets. Many of these shops and centers are non-

This bathroom is designed with a recycle center in mind. Hollywood lights, medicine cabinets, cabinets with counters, and cast-iron sinks with built-in backsplashes are salvaged materials that can be readily found at most recycle centers.

This sun-filled master bathroom speaks to what this book is all about—incorporating salvaged materials in a way that is both aesthetically pleasing and highly functional. A salvaged tub, vintage windows from a public building, and salvaged floors work together to create an inviting haven for a relaxing bath.

profit organizations. They usually take more common building materials than architectural shops do. It is important to get to know the folks at these places as well; many amazing things come through their doors—2 x 2-inch slate tiles from an old patio, library slider doors, extra decking pieces that can be used for cabinetry, bricks from a walkway that can be used for a fireplace, plain white ceramic tiles that can be hand painted pieces. The centers are also great places for training, back-to-work programs, and community centers.

Specialty Shops

Many companies create products out of salvaged materials. Recycled aluminum hardware and sinks, vintage lighting and restored lighting, glass tiles and salvaged wood pieces—these are just a few examples of the types of products many local small businesses can provide for you. Find out who is in your

area and work with local companies to help you put together your salvaged materials list.

Fairs and Flea Markets

What better way is there to spend a sunny Saturday than wandering through an outdoor flea market? Many of the booths in these markets are rented by dealers on a weekly basis, but sometimes people rent them for just a weekend to get rid of stuff stored in their attic or garage. With the advent of eBay, most people now have a sense of what the items they've selling are worth, but sometimes you can find real steals at flea markets.

Antique fairs are also good places to look. Most of the vendors at fairs are dealers, many of them with their own shops, so be sure to pick up business cards from vendors you like so you can visit their shop later. Fairs and flea markets generally have items that are more transportable—things like stained glass windows, lighting fixtures, hardware, and tables.

▲ Here is another example of how salvaged materials can be used in place of a built-in structure. These old wooden boxes have been put together and framed around the edge to create an instant closet. Salvaged metal pipes are used for hanging racks.

▸ Functional and attractive, these shelving units salvaged from a retail video store now play a key role in a small country kitchen for a large family.

The Internet: eBay and Craigslist

The Internet is a great place to find businesses that sell salvaged materials—most shops and centers have their own website. And eBay and Craigslist, of

Moist
Deluxe
Salada

course, are used by thousands of people everyday. But the Internet is also a place to be wary of. Only use reputable websites, check seller ratings when they are available, do not give your personal information, do not accept checks if you are selling, and always feel comfortable saying no.

The best way to find salvaged materials is to stick to your surrounding area and see if a neighbor or someone in a nearby town is selling what you are looking for. Homeowners who have leftover stone, tile, or wood from their own projects or have architectural pieces they are taking out of their home often try to sell them on local websites like Craigslist or front-yard forums.

Used Equipment Warehouses

Most people aren't aware that large universities have warehouse sales or that restaurant closeouts can mean amazing deals on stoves, refrigerators, stainless-steel equipment, and more. Corporations or businesses and hotels that are remodeling, relocating, or going out of business often sell office equipment and furniture at great prices. Keep a list of locations that are near you and what they usually offer so you can give them a call when you are looking or stop by to see what they have in stock that day. The great thing about these salvage warehouses is that new items are brought in regularly.

This is where some good detective work comes into play. The most unique salvaged pieces can often come from the most unusual places. For example, if the town you live in has a university, they will likely have warehouse where they store leftover classroom supplies or materials from a past renovation. In an effort to divest themselves of these old supplies, universities may sell the items from time to time, so keep an eye out for such sales. Think outside the box and you may not only finding interesting building materials, but unique design items as well.

Building Professionals and Construction Sites

Although I don't advise you to go dumpster-diving on someone's private property when you see a construction project happening, you can—and should—consider building professionals and construction sites as a source for salvaged materials. If you do see something in or near a dumpster, ask the builder or

◂ Who would have thought that leftover decking pieces from a construction site could look so good as a bathroom vanity? Concrete floors made with salvaged aggregate and a stunning walk-in shower make this small bathroom look larger than life. The homeowner painted the cabinetry with high-gloss boat paint to give it that special shine and to protect it from wear and water.

▸ You are only limited to your imagination. This fun staircase was made from colorful salvaged tiles that were broken and turned into mosaics. The railing was made from a variety of metal objects. The door at the top of the stairs was also salvaged and the stair treads are from pickle barrels.

homeowner if you can have it and let that person get it out for you. More and more builders are recycling much of their construction debris, so another option is to find out where they are sending it or even ask if you can take it off their hands before it heads off. Be respectful if they choose to send it to a non-profit recycle center first. This is helpful for the homeowner as a tax write-off and for the recycle center's profit.

10 TIPS FOR YOUR SALVAGE SEARCH

1. Make a list of things you need before you go so you don't forget: doors, fixtures, and knobs (how many?), sinks, flooring (how much square footage?). You can even include things you still aren't sure about: an island or cabinets beneath a counter? tin or stone tiles for the wall behind the woodstove?
2. Don't be overwhelmed and give yourself enough time to look through everything twice—you'll always see more the second time around.
3. Remember to see beyond the items in their current form—what you are looking at doesn't have to be the final product. Use your imagination!
4. Bring a friend with you. Searching through salvage shops can be daunting, so it's nice to have a second opinion, especially when you are considering more costly items.
5. If you want a salvaged item to be refinished, recut, rebuilt, or rewired, ask the shop owner about it. He or she will often be able to help you transform the salvage material or will know someone else who can.
6. Ask for help. Not sure if the hinges you want to buy match the door you have? Wondering whether the window you are looking at is double-hung or tempered glass, or if the wood you are considering would be good for floors? Is that sink enamel or porcelain? What kind of sealant does that stone need? Shop owners and employees are usually very knowledgeable about the items they sell.
7. Prices are sometimes negotiable. It is helpful if you have an idea of pricing for a particular kind of item, as well as a good sense of budget allowances.
8. Looking for something specific? Ask the shop owners if they have it. Many shops and centers have other storage locations or facilities, or a network of people they work with who can help them search out a particular item for you. Even if they can't find it immediately, they can keep an eye out and call you if they come across it. Just keep checking in.
9. Keep coming back. New things arrive every day, and you don't want to miss that perfect vanity or pile of slate shingles.
10. Have fun—and know that when you purchase salvaged material, you are bringing character, history, and an earth-friendly statement into your home.

◂ This sunny cottage-style kitchen has countertops that not only are stylish but affordable, too. These salvaged countertops were less expensive than common laminate.

Putting It All Together

A PORTFOLIO OF DESIGN CONCEPTS

The goal of this book is to give you a sense of the wide range of salvaged material available, as well as the unique and unusual places to find it. But what about putting it all together? As with any kind of design, forethought and planning are paramount when creating interiors, especially when you are using salvaged or one-of-a-kind recycled pieces. This chapter provides a visual cornucopia of the different looks that can be achieved using salvage. With some basic design foresight, you can put together an interior in any style you desire—clean and contemporary, funky and eclectic, elegant and sophisticated, rustic and charming.

A salvaged vintage door balances out new cabinetry.

THE BIG PICTURE

Like a painter, you start with a blank canvas. The walls, floors, and ceilings are the backdrops for your tables, islands, furniture, and lighting, and their character will affect the look of everything else you put in the room. For example, an oval-shaped, candy-apple-red enamel sink in a well-lit bathroom might look fun and quirky next to a wall covered in hand-painted tiles, but it could just as easily look sleek and seductive against a dark-slate sink top and ebony-stained walls lit with wall sconces. Knowing how the different materials will interact visually will affect the design decisions you make. If your floors are made of salvaged vintage lumber with a distinctive look, take that into consideration when designing the rest of the room. You might choose to go with an open floor plan that shows off the floors, or, if that's not possible, you might select furniture that allows people to see the floor beneath it. If the walls are going play center stage with broken pieces of pottery as the tile work, the rest of the room should be simple and clean to create a balance. By taking this approach, you create a home that is easy to move through visually, with each room flowing coherently into the next.

BALANCE IS KEY

It's easy to fall in love with all salvaged material; it's a lot harder to find the right balance of pieces and materials in a room. Size, texture, shape, color, level of detail—all play a role in establishing the character of the individual piece or material. And once you've put those pieces and materials together in a room, all those elements will contribute to the visual conversation.

To avoid creating a mishmash of salvaged items that fight for the spotlight in your home, take some time to decide which pieces should be allowed to take center stage and which are better as accent details. Painted dimensional

The louver doors pictured here were salvaged from the master-bedroom closets during renovation. The homeowner had them repainted to match the media room walls and then umber-washed them to give an antique look.

▸ These doors, made with salvaged lumber and metal, are simple in their design. Their size and shape give this entranceway a "wow" appeal.

lumber can be used as wall wainscoting in a master bathroom, but it shouldn't outshine the gorgeous vintage tub in the middle of the room. Do the doors complement the trim, or are they competing for attention? Multicolored tile works well with solid-colored counters and cabinets because the solid color provides a visual break from the activity of the tile. And if you want the Victorian-era chandelier you purchased for the dining room to really stand out, it would be a good idea to consider a simple design for the rest of the space. Balancing your salvaged pieces and materials is just as important as finding the items themselves, and striking the right balance between centerpieces and accent details separates the nice homes from the amazing ones.

PROPORTION

Proportion is one of the most important components of balance. A gigantic island created from a salvaged store counter can make an amazing statement in a kitchen. But adding two extra-large vintage chandeliers from an old theater above it would make the space feel too crowded. (Plus, it is best to have three lights over an island, not two.) At the other extreme, pendant lights made from old canning jars would look puny over the large island. But they might be perfect in a small bungalow kitchen. Another example: If you have large, exposed wooden beams in the living-room ceiling, be careful not to fill the room with a lot of heavy, oversized pieces of salvaged wood. Unless you're designing a mountainside log cabin, too many heavy wood pieces can feel oppressive.

WHERE TO START?

Designing a room is a little like coming up with a good physical-workout routine: You first start with the larger muscles (or design components) and then work your way to the smaller ones. For example, if you are designing a kitchen, you should first consider the character of the walls, floors, and cabinetry, then move to the midsized components like countertops and sinks, and, finally, choose the small details like hardware. That said, if you are really in love with a stack of tiles you found at a salvage center or the hardware you discovered at an antique shop, you can instead work small to big, choosing cabinets that will look right with the knobs, and walls and floors that will complement the cabinets.

A good rule of thumb is to know your priorities. If the drawer pulls are what's most important to you, design the room around them. If you have your heart set on a towering stone fireplace surround, choose flooring and furniture that doesn't compete with it but also isn't overshadowed by the big-statement piece. Of course, knowing your priorities sometimes means making compromises. You may love the marble countertops and the hand-painted tiles that would fit perfectly as a backsplash and those 1950s glass globes for pendant lights, but if they don't work together, you're going to have to eliminate one of them. The good news is that whatever doesn't make the cut in one room can probably be made to fit somewhere else, perhaps with a little refinishing or other alterations.

Putting your whole design together before you begin installation ensures a good outcome, allowing you to see if the pieces you've chosen will work together structurally, functionally, and aesthetically. If the material is easily transportable, such as a tile, take it with you when you're searching for the other components of the room. Bring pictures of the space you are designing and the room measurements on your salvage hunts. And, of course, don't forget your tape measure—there's nothing more frustrating than realizing that the perfect sideboard you bought for the bathroom won't actually fit in it!

TAKING CHANCES

As in any kind of design, there will be times when you just don't get it right. When working with salvaged material, especially one-of-a-kind pieces, the process and results will be new to everyone, including the architect and builder. But what is life without a little risk? When you walk into a space and it "wows" you, it's because the architect, designer, or homeowner took a chance. Be prepared for mistakes, but know that most of the time you'll get it right.

A beautifully designed, finished room isn't the only reward in working with salvaged material—the initial inspiration, the hunt, the selection, and the anticipation you feel as you watch the room come together are all a part of the fun. And, of course, knowing that your eco-friendly process is contributing to the greater good of the world makes it just that much better.

It's easy to see how you could incorporate these beautiful salvaged glass globes into your home design.

▲ A dining room with wainscoting made from salvaged doors, globe lighting, and vintage salvaged French doors.

▶ The glass in this salvaged mudroom-entranceway door was removed and replaced with copper panels for privacy. The old glass sash brings in light from outside.

End cuts of timber from an old dam make the floor of this home a show-stopper. End-cut flooring can be very time-consuming and difficult to install, but it is well worth the trouble. Each piece is like a work of art, with its own fingerprint of growth rings and color.

Here an old newel post and railing accent a simple stair system, which is a visible feature in the open floor plan of the living room. A great example of using salvage as a highlight rather than the main attraction. Also note the salvaged beam used as an accent piece leading upstairs.

FARAH
COOKBOOK
HAROLD McGEE
All About Braising
THE BARBECUE! BIBLE
THE NEW BASICS COOKBOOK
COOK'S ILLUSTRATED 2007
SOMEWHERE OVER THE RAINBOW
Gallery

▲ The doors in this upstairs hallway make a design statement in addition to being functional. They were stripped and left unfinished, letting the character of the wood speak for itself.

◀ This mini office space in a kitchen uses salvaged chalkboard. The family left it unoiled so that messages could be written directly on the counter itself.

A combination of tile and stone pieces in a geometric pattern. It is easier to find a few leftover pieces than a lot of one material. Take advantage of the different sizes and shapes and create your own pattern. The salvaged transom windows on either side of the fireplace add some fun lighting.

Even strike plates for doors can be salvaged. There is practically no home material that can't be found in a salvaged or recycled state.

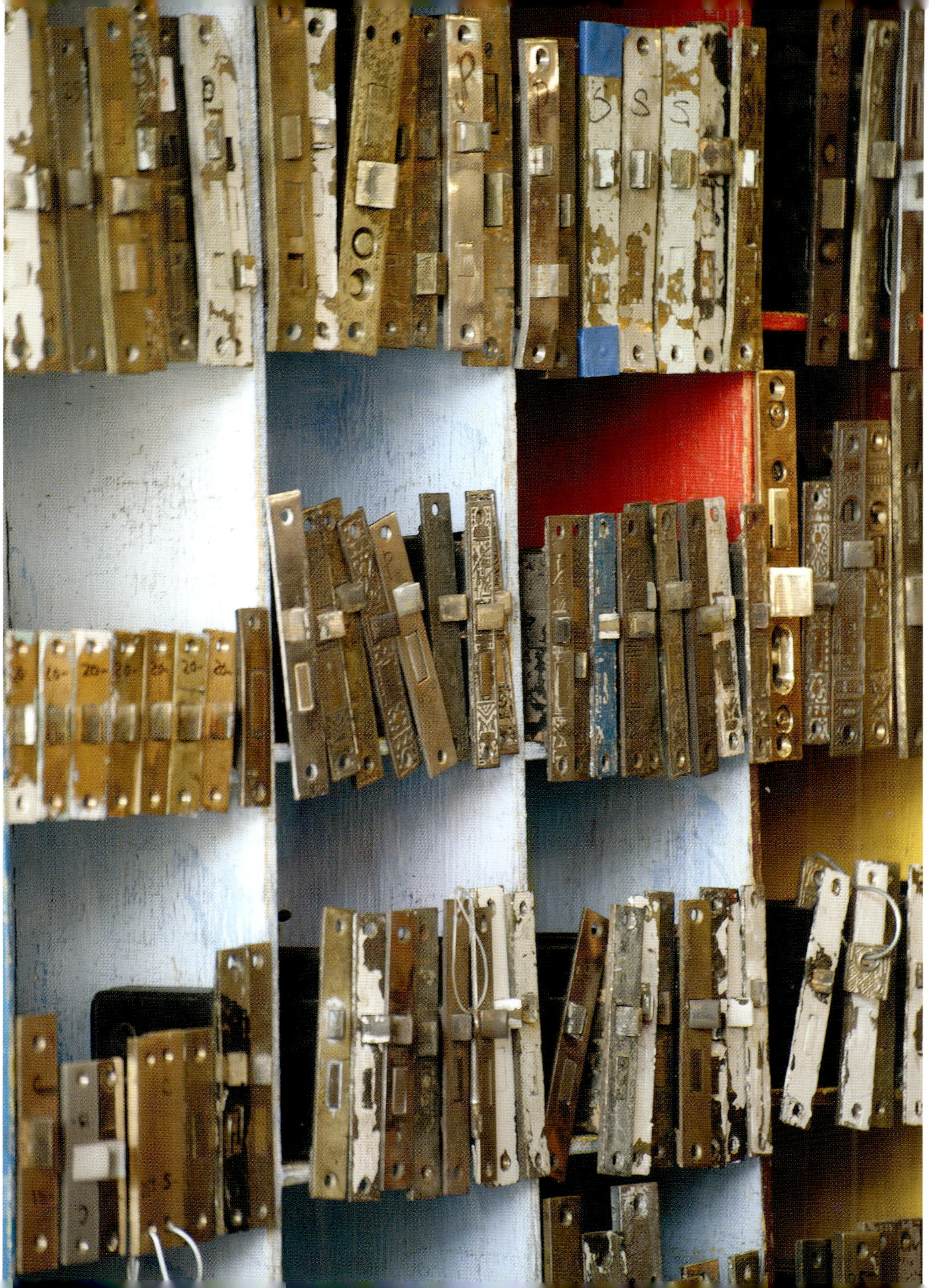

▸ Vintage stained glass that lets light into a bathroom without losing privacy.

▸▸ These interesting metal pieces are waiting at a lighting shop to be reborn into light fixtures.

◀ This classic room features salvaged columns, beams, and trim work on the mantel. These elements blend beautifully with the antiques in the room.

◀◀ The kitchen pictured here is a wonderful example of mixed salvaged wood. The cabinets on the right were salvaged from a rebuilding shop and installed without refinishing to honor the old-growth trees they are made of. The island on the left is a mix of salvaged wood made into cabinets, with a top piece of maple that was once part of a stage at a Waldorf school.

◂ Mismatched salvaged doors make an interesting entrance for a home office.

◂◂ A stunning timber-framed home with a cathedral ceiling uses salvaged flooring from a torn-down factory building.

▲ As this illustration shows, mixing elegant salvaged items with leftover construction material can make for a striking design. This salvaged claw-foot tub rests on a bed of concrete blocks while a vintage chandelier hangs above. The wood flooring could be left in its natural color with a high-gloss finish, and the wall of dimensional lumber could be whitewashed to soften the room.

▶ The pantry door seen here is an old barn door purchased at an architectural salvage shop. The homeowner painted right over the green with a red paint (the same color they used for the island). The green bleeds through, producing a weathered, textured look. Metal brackets at the top allow the door to easily slide open and shut, taking up less space than a conventional swing door.

▲ Salvaged chandeliers are pieces of hanging art. From decadent to minimalist, the choices in style are endless, as are the places you can use them.

▶ This salvaged barn door with its original slider rail is used to separate a family room from the great room.

▲ A mudroom is always a bonus in a house, but sometimes due to space or budget constraints, a full-blown built-in is not possible. This drawing shows how easy it is to get a fun design—and extra space—with a little effort. Use salvaged boards as a wall panel with door knobs as hooks. Find some old milk crates for storage and seating while putting on shoes, and add a salvaged stone floor with a mosaic in the middle.

◄ This garage is made of salvaged board from a neighboring barn that was deconstructed.

Something as simple as salvaged tile pieces under a modern woodstove can give a room a big punch of style. Worked into the clay floor, the reclaimed European tiles seen here give the appearance of a rug while being fire-resistant.

A salvaged screen built into the wall of this mountain retreat gives the homeowner a little privacy in bed and allows for airflow. The floors in the home are salvaged Douglas fir from an old barn.

◀ The dark wood of this vintage sideboard, which functions as a bathroom vanity, stands up nicely to the bold colors of the tile work. The vintage lighting adds to the room's elegance. The high legs of the vanity give the room a larger feel by allowing a peek at the wall underneath.

▶ This entranceway to a ski chalet was created with plywood—an excellent example of how you can incorporate salvaged plywood into your own design.

▲ Salvaged stone pieces can be left in their purchased state and pushed together to create an abstract fireplace surround. With large salvaged granite steps as the hearth, this gas-insert fireplace has a modern edge that is also very dramatic.

▶ Salvaged glass doors add detail to the upper cabinets of this shelf system. The tiles below it were hand-painted and sealed to protect the paint.

▸ These kitchen cabinets are 15 inches long—the size of the salvaged pieces of IPE decking material. When designing your home, think about how you can use the inherent qualities of the salvaged material to best effect. IPE decking, for example, is fairly heavy, and heavy wood is great for cabinetry because it weighs it down, making the drawers slide open more easily. The refrigerator in this kitchen was salvaged from a friend's home; the front piece was once green but the homeowner removed the panel and updated it. The slate tiles and small white tile were both leftover from a client's bathroom project. The ceiling consists of salvaged closet dowel rods. The ceiling trusses are salvaged dimensional lumber, left exposed to show the character of the pieces.

▸▸ Doors are one of the most common structural elements available. When considering salvaged doors, plan ahead because every door is different and you will need to build the door jambs to fit. Doors can also be used as a variety of other interior design elements—headboards, wainscoting, tables, screens, and so on. You can be as creative as the door designs themselves.

▸ Popular especially in the Northeast are salvaged metal grates built right into entranceway porches, or even in mudroom floors. These grates not only give a punch of design detail but also are helpful for stamping off mud, sand, or snow before entering the home. Grates usually have a lip around the edge and need to be carefully measured before the porch is constructed. Some are able to be screwed down into the porch itself, so you can lift it to clean out the leaves and mud at anytime. The vintage ceiling light in this mudroom emits a warm glow in the evening, welcoming guests in.

▸▸ These dining room cabinets are salvaged 2x6 Douglas fir studs from an old building with an oil finish. The salvaged alder counter has a living edge, and marks from the bolts and nails that were once in it give a sense of the history of the wood.

▸ The REX Project, mentioned in Chapter 6, is an excellent example of a home that uses salvaged material. Homeowner Shannon Quimby repurposed the condemned home and used 99% of the material in her new home. The open floor plan allows you to see all the unique salvaged materials at a glance—the newel post, flooring, island counter, salvaged glass in the countertop, wainscoting on the island, window transom, creative dining-room and island light fixtures, vintage fixture above the sink, and much more. Today's kitchen can use yesterday's material.

▸▸ This country-home entrance is just the beginning of the salvage finds in this home. The brick and the vintage door and knocker are both salvaged and make a wonderfully welcoming first impression.

Vintage glass cabinet doors and stained glass pieces are simple salvage additions that make big impressions.

Resources

The following resources were consulted in the creation of this book. A list of additional resources for readers searching out salvage and the people who work with it follows.

ARCHITECTS, DESIGNERS, AND BUILDERS

Arciform
Portland, Oregon
503-493-7344
www.arciform.com

DRW Design/Build
Portland, Oregon
503-577-2824
www.drwdesignbuild.com

Nathan Good Architects
Portland, Oregon; Salem, Oregon
503-507-4116
www.nathangoodarchitects.com

Gristmill Builders
Stowe, Vermont
802-253-6393
www.gristmillbuilders.com

Jim Huntington Design/Build
Charlotte, Vermont
802-578-3408
www.jimhuntingtondesignbuild.com

Peregrine Design/Build
Cliff Deetjen, Architect
Burlington, Vermont
802-383-1808
www.peregrinedesignbuild.com

Shannon Quimby, Interior Designer, Speaker, Television Host
The REX Project (Reuse Everything Experiment)
Portland, Oregon
www.shannonquimby.com

SALVAGE SOURCES AND SERVICES

Bedrock Industries (recycled glass and recycled glass products)
Seattle, Washington
206-283-7625
www.bedrockindustries.com

Conant Metal and Light (repurposed lighting)
Burlington, Vermont
802-658-4482
www.conantmetalandlight.com

Eleek (recycled metal lights, sinks, hardware)
Portland, Oregon
503-232-5526
www.eleek.com

Gleenglass
Vancouver, Washington
360-882-0629
www.gleenglass.com

Hippo Hardware & Trading Company
Portland, Oregon
503-231-1444
www.hippohardware.com

Mason Brothers Architectural Salvage Warehouse
Essex, Vermont
802-879-4221
www.greatsalvage.com

ReBUILD (a program of ReSOURCE)
Burlington, Vermont
802-846-4007
www.rebuildvt.org

Rebuilding Center of Our United Villages
Portland, Oregon
503-331-1877
www.rebuldingcenter.org

Red Concrete
Burlington, Vermont
802-862-3676
www.redconcrete.com

ADDITIONAL RESOURCES: ARCHITECTS, DESIGNERS, AND BUILDERS

Heidi Arnold Design
340-514-0072
www.heidiarnolddesign.com

Sarah Barnard Design
Los Angeles, California
818-988-8821
www.sarahbarnard.com

Batt + Lear, Designers and Builders
Seattle, Washington
206-301-1999
www.battandlear.com

Bent Architecture
Boston, Massachusetts
617-513-5784
www.bentarchitecture.com

Birdseye Architecture & Building
Richmond, Vermont
802-434-2112
www.birdseyebuilding.co

Conner and Buck Builders
Bristol, Vermont
802-453-2756
www.connerandbuck.com

Cowey de Vasselot Architects
Paris, France

Cushman Design Group
Stowe, Vermont
802-253-2169
www.cushmandesign.com

CWC Company
Carrie Wulfman
Middlebury, Vermont
802-388-1846
cwulfman@sover.net

Czopek & Erdenberger Inc.
Portland, Oregon
503-242-0956
www.czopek.com

Aidlin Darling Design
San Francisco, California
415-974-5603
www.aidlindarlingdesign.com

Doerr Architecture
Thomas Doerr
Boulder, Colorado
303-544-0209
www.doerr.org

Echo Studio
Chicago, Illinois
312-316-7464
www.echostudiochicago.com

Rich Elstrom Construction
Gearhart, Oregon
503-738-0274
www.richelstromconstruction.com

Fivecat Studio
Pleasantville, New York
914-747-1177
www.fivecat.com

Green Hammer Design & Build
Portland, Oregon
503-804-1746
www.greenhammerconstruction.com

Green Leaf Builder
Newton, Massachusetts
617-558-8811
www.greenleafbuilderllc.com

Greenleaf Construction, Inc.
Bothell, Washington
425-712-9014

Gyllenborg Construction
Morrisville, Vermont
802-888-9288

Frank Harmon Architect
Raleigh, North Carolina
919-829-9464
www.frankharmon.com

Elizabeth Herrmann Architecture + Design
Bristol, Vermont
802-453-6401
www.eharchitect.com

David Hertz Architects, Inc.
Santa Monica, California
310-829-9932
www.studioea.com

Jim Huntington, Design/Build
Charlotte, Vermont
802-578-3408
www.jimhuntingtondesignbuild.com

Integrity Construction Inc.
Bob Coates and Jim Kilcoyne
Winooski, Vermont
802-373-7334

Interstice Architects
San Francisco, California
415-285-3960
www.intersticearchitects.com

Phil Kean Designs
Winter Park, Florida
407-599-3922
www.philkeandesigns.com

Neil Kelly Design/Build/Remodeling
Janel Campbell
Portland, Oregon; Lake Oswego, Oregon;
Bend, Oregon; Eugene, Oregon
866-691-2719
www.neilkelly.com

Kendle Design Collaborative
Scottsdale, Arizona
480-951-8558
www.kendledesign.com

Karin Lidbeck-Brent
Woodbury, Connecticut
www.lidbeckbrent.com

Lewis Creek Builders
North Ferrisburg, Vermont
802-999-6942
802-355-0271
www.lewiscreekbuilders.com

John McLeod Architect
Middlebury, Vermont
917-531-2121
www.johnmcleodarchitect.com

Laura Migliori & Peter Brevig, Architects
Portland, Oregon
503-228-4921

Michael Minadeo + Partners
Essex Junction, Vermont
802-540-0055
www.minadeopartners.com

Mitra Designs Studio, Inc.
Bristol, Vermont
802-453-5438
www.mitradesigns.com

North Woods Joinery
Cambridge, Vermont
802-644-2400
www.nwjoinery.com

Northern Timbers Construction
Ripton, Vermont
802-388-0132
www.northerntimbers.com

Pill-Maharam Architects
Shelburne, Vermont
802-735-1286
www.pillmaharam.com

Dave Rush Design, Build, Remodel
Portland, Oregon
503-460-9212
www.rushtobuild.com

Sam Scofield, Architect
Stowe, Vermont
802-253-9948
www.samscofieldarchitect.com

Linnia Sayers
Summerland Style
Bellingham, Washington
360-223-6427
www.summerandstyle.com

Selin + Selin Architecture
Shelburne, Vermont
802-985-0127
www.selinandselin.com

Silver Maple Construction LLC
Bristol, Vermont
802-453-7767
www.silvermapleconstruction.com

Silver Ridge Design, Inc. Architects
Hyde Park, Vermont
802-888-2400
www.silverridgedesign.com

South Village Sales Gallery & Design Center
South Burlington, Vermont
802-861-7600
www.southvillage.com

Studio III Architects
Gregory C. Masefield Jr., AIA
802-453-3286
gregorm@gmavt.net

Sweeney Design Build
Shelburne, Vermont
802-985-1070
www.sweeneydesignbuild.com

TruexCullins Architects & Interiors
Burlington, Vermont
802-658-2775
www.truexcullins.com

urbanminers, llc
Joseph DeRisi
Hamden, Connecticut
203-287-0852
www.urbanminers.com

Urban Spruce Residential, Hospitality, and Commercial Interior Design
Laura Takashima
Lake Oswego, Oregon
503-901-5757
www.urbanspruce.com

Dennis Wedlick Architect, LLC
New York, New York
212-625-9222
www.denniswedlick.com

SALVAGE SOURCES AND OTHER SERVICES

Adkins Architectural Antiques
Houston, Texas
713-522-6547
www.adkinsantiques.com

Admac Salvage
Littleton, New Hampshire
603-444-1200
www.admacsalvage.com

American Barn Company
Chicago, Illinois
773-327-1560
www.americanbarncompany.com

Amighini Architectural
Jersey City, New Jersey
201-222-6367
www.amighini.net

Architectural Antiquities
Harborside, Maine
207-326-4938
www.archantiquities.com

Architectural Artifacts
Chicago, Illinois
773-348-0622
www.architecturalartifacts.com

Architectural Heritage
Birmingham, Alabama
205-322-3538
www.architecturalheritage.com

Architectural Salvage, Inc.
Exeter, New Hampshire
603-773-5635
www.oldhousesalvage.com

Architectural Salvage Warehouse
Burlington, Vermont
802-658-5011
www.architecturalsalvagevt.com

Boston Building Material Co-op
Boston, Massachusetts
617-442-2262
www.bbmc.com

The Brass Knob Architectural Antiques
Washington, DC
202-332-3370
www.thebrassknob.com

Build It Green
Astoria, New York
718-777-0132
www.bignyc.com

Building ReSources
San Francisco, California
415-285-7814
www.buildingresources.org

Champlain Valley Antique Center
Shelburne, Vermont
802-985-8116

Church Hill Landscaping (masonry)
Charlotte, Vermont
802-425-5222
www.churchhilllandscapes.com

City Lights Antique Lighting
Cambridge, Massachusetts
617-547-1490
www.citylights.nu

City Salvage
Minneapolis, Minnesota
612-627-9107
www.citysalvage.com

Community Forklift Salvage
Edmonston, Maryland
301-985-5180
www.communityforklift.com

Construction Junction
Pittsburgh, Pennsylvania
412-243-5025
www.constructionjunction.org

Crown City Hardware
Pasadena, California
626-794-0234
www.crowncityhardware.com

The Demolition Depot
New York, New York
212-860-1138
www.demolitiondepot.com

Dennis & Company, Inc.
Portland, Oregon
503-637-5177

Discount Home Warehouse Architectural Salvage
Dallas, Texas
214-631-2755
www.dhsalvage.com

Earthwise Building Salvage
Seattle, Washington
206-624-4510
www.earthwise-salvage.com

Ecohaus
San Francisco, California; Seattle, Washington;
Portland, Oregon
877-432-6428
www.ecohaus.com

Marty Eichinger Studio
Portland, Oregon
503-223-0626
www.eichingersculpture.com

Endurawood
Portland, Oregon
503-233-7090
www.endurawood.com

Eugenia's Antique Hardware
Chamblee, Georgia
770-458-1677
www.eugeniaantiquehardware.com

Foundation Architectual Reclamation
Kansas City, Missouri
816-283-8990
www.foundationkc.com

Hippo Hardware & Trading Company
Portland, Oregon
503-231-1444
www.hippohardware.com

Historic Houseparts
Rochester, New York
888-558-2329
www.historichouseparts.com

Housewerks Architectural Werkshop
Baltimore, Maryland
410-685-8047
www.housewerksalvage.com

Irreplaceable Artifacts
Middletown, Connecticut
860-344-85-76
www.irreplaceableartifacts.com

The Lamp Shop
Burlington, Vermont
802-864-6782
www.thelampshopvt.com

The Loading Dock
Baltimore, Maryland
410-558-3625
www.loadingdock.org

LooLoo Design
Portsmouth, Rhode Island
800-508-0022
www.looloodesign.com

Mason Brothers Architectural Salvage Warehouse
Essex Junction, Vermont
802-879-4221
www.greatsalvage.com

Materials Unlimited
Ypsilanti, Minnesota
800-299-9462
www.materialsunlimited.com

Melange Antiques and Architecturals
Sunset, Louisiana
888-662-5151
www.melangeantiques.com

Muddy Creek Stone Company
Vermont
802-877-9291

New England Demolition and Salvage
New Bedford, Massachusetts
508-992-1099
www.nedsalvage.com

North Shore Architectural Antiques
Two Harbors, Minnesota
218-834-0018
www.north-shore-architectural-antiques.com

Ohmega Salvage General Store
Berkeley, California
510-204-0767
www.ohmegasalvage.com

Old House Parts Company
Kennebunk, Maine
207-985-1999
www.oldhouseparts.com

Old Portland Hardware & Architectural
Portland, Oregon
503-234-7380
www.oldportlandhardware.com

Olde Good Things
Los Angeles, California
213-746-8600
New York, New York
212-989-8814
Scranton, Pennsylvania
570-341-7668
www.ogtstore.com

Pasadena Architectural Salvage
Pasadena, California
626-535-9655
www.pasadenaarchitecturalsalvage.com

Portland Architectural Salvage
Portland, Maine
207-780-0634
www.portlandsalvage.com

ReBUILD Vermont
Burlington, Vermont
802-846-4015
www.rebuildvt.org

The ReBuilding Center
Portland, Oregon
503-331-1877
www.rebuildingcenter.org

ReBuilding Exchange
Chicago, Illinois
773-847-3761
www.rebuildingexchange.org

The ReCONNstruction Center
New Britain, Connecticut
860-597-3390
www.reconnstructioncenter.org

Recycling the Past
Barnegat, New Jersey
609-660-9790
www.recyclingthepast.com

Rejuvenation
Seattle, Washington
206-382-1901
Portland, Oregon
503-238-1900
www.rejuvenation.com

Resource
Boulder, Colorado
303-419-5418
www.resourceyard.org

Restoration Resources
Boston, Massachusetts
617-542-3033
www.restorationresources.com

The RE Store
Seattle, Washington
206-297-9119
www.re-store.org

The ReUse Center
Ann Arbor, Michigan
734-222-7880
www.recycleannarbor.org

Ricca's Demolishing Corp.
New Orleans, Louisiana
504-488-5524
www.riccaarchitectural.com

Salvage Heaven
Milwaukee, Wisconsin
414-482-0286
www.salvageheaven.com

Salvage New York
Jersey City, New Jersey
201-222-6367
www.salvagenewyork.com

Salvage One
Chicago, Illinois
312-733-0098
www.salvageone.com

Santa Fe Wrecking Company
Los Angeles, California
213-765-8166
www.santafewrecking.net

Sarasota Architectural Salvage
Sarasota, Florida
941-362-0803
www.collectibledetective.com

Second Use Building Materials
Seattle, Washington
206-763-6929
www.seconduse.com

Sierra Pacific Windows
(multiple locations)
800-824-7744
www.sierrapacificwindows.com

Shoreham Upholstery
Jim Ortuno and Ethan McArdle
Shoreham, Vermont
802-897-5711
www.shorehamupholstery.com

Southern Accents Architectural Antiques
Cullman, Alabama
205-737-0554
www.antiques-architectural.com

Standard Supply Company, Inc.
Portland, Oregon
800-929-5039
www.standardsupplyco.com

Taipan Architectural Salvage
Santa Barbara, California
805-845-5625
www.taipanarchsalvage.com

TreeForm Woodwork
Eric McClelland
Portland, Oregon
503-880-8903
www.treeformwoodwork.com

West End Architectural Salvage
Des Moines, Iowa
515-243-0499
www.westendarchsalvage.com

White River Architectural Salvage and Antiques
Centerville, Indiana

800-262-3389
www.whiteriversalvage.com

Whole Building Company Supply & Salvage
East Palo Alto, California
650-328-8731
www.driftwoodsalvage.com

Woodcrafters
Portland, Oregon
800-777-3709
www.woodcrafters.us

Yolo Colorhouse
(multiple locations)
www.yolocolorhouse.com

DIRECTORIES AND DO-IT-YOURSELF WEBSITES

Directory of Architectural Salvage Stores
www.oldhousejournal.com

Directory of Recycled Building Materials
www.ecobusinesslinks.com

Directory of ReUse People
www.thereusepeople.org

Other Helpful Sites
www.doityourself.com

www.askthebuilder.com

www.greenhomebuilding.com

www.webecoist.com

Index

Note: Page numbers in italic type indicate photographs or illustrations.

A

N

O

P

Q

R

S

Credits

Below is a list, by page number, of the designers who allowed us to photograph their work for inclusion in the book. We appreciate their support and commitment to salvaging material so we may live more gently on our planet.

Front cover, pp. 52, 65, 82, 87, 93, 97, 200, 207, 214, 223, 224, 231, 238: designer, Heidi Arnold Design & Gristmill Builders

Opposite title page (recycled glass), p. 22: DES-SYN, South Village, Vermont

Copyright page, pp. 14, 25, 67, 91, 105 (old store counter from Mason Brothers Architectural Salvage), 143, 147, 155, 157, 175, 191, 237: designer, Carrie Wulfman, CWC Company; builder, Robert Anderson

pp. 6, 47, 101, 111, 114, 118, 123: The ReBuilding Center, Portland, Oregon

pp. 9, 15, 58, 150, 163 and 165 (light fixtures, The Lamp Shop), 198, 210, 234: designer, homeowner and Jim Huntington; builder, Jim Huntington Design Build

pp. 10, 68, 188, 211: designer, Joanne Palmisano; architect, Silver Ridge Design; builder, Jim Huntington Design Build

pp. 12, 18, 50, 100, 124 (right), 128, 135, 197, 228: Arciform Design Build

pp. 16, 21, 122, 125, 134, 137: designer, Joanne Palmisano; builder, Jim Huntington Design Build

pp. 20, 39, 162, 164, 176: architect, Michael Minadeo & Partners; builder, Integrity Construction

pp. 23 (concrete sink), 79 (left, counters): Red Concrete, Burlington, Vermont

pp. 26, 49, 51, 60, 129, 149, 203, 209: designer, homeowner and Conner & Buck Design Build

pp. 27, 38, 117 and 145 (with designer, Joanne Palmisano), 189: The ReBuild Center, Burlington, Vermont

p. 28, 30, 77, 83, 84, 98, 116, 130: interior designer, Georgia Erdenberger, Czopek & Erdenberger; architect, Nathan Good Architects

pp. 32, 33, 70, 108, 110, 115, 151, 193, 208, 227: designer, homeowner

pp. 34, 56, 71, 73, 107, 119. 122 (top), 154, 156, 184–186, 233: Mason Brothers Architectural Salvage, Essex Junction, Vermont

pp. 35, 43, 138: architect, Gregory Masefield, Studio III Architects; builder, Silver Maple Construction

pp. 37, 113, 124 (left), 152, 194, 232: architect, Ryan Walsh, DRW Design/Build

pp. 41, 95: designer, Marty Eichinger, Eichinger Sculpture Studio

pp. 42, 121, 159: designer, Mitra Design Studio; builder, Conner & Buck Design Build

p. 44: designer, The Cushman Design Group; builder, Gyllenborg Construction

pp. 45, 88, 103, 126, 161, 201: designer, Laura Hollister-Takashima, Hunter Lane Interiors; architect, Simon Tompkinson; builder, Dave Rush Design & Build

pp. 46, 48, 66, 80, 96, 153, 166, 169, 187, 236: designer, Shannon Quimby; builder, The Green Hammer

pp. 54, 218: architect, Sam Scofield and North Woods Joinery

pp. 57, 148: Conner & Buck Design Build

p. 59: designer, Joanne Palmisano, Peregrine Design Build

pp. 61, 90, 112, 139, 146, 170, 190, 192, 206, 212, 220, 225, 230: design idea, Joanne Palmisano; drawing, Cliff Deetjen

p. 63: architect, Pill-Maharam Architects; builder, Conner & Buck Design Build

pp. 72, 74: Jim Huntington Design Build

p. 75: architect, Elizabeth Herrmann Architecture & Design

pp. 78, 85: countertop, Gleenglass; designer, Jane Campbell, Neil Kelly Design/Build/Remodeling

p. 79, right: salvaged glass, Bedrock Industries

p. 86: designer, homeowner; salvaged glass tiles, Bedrock Industries

pp. 89, 167, 205, 213, 222: Hippo Hardware, Portland, Oregon

p. 102: architect, Geoffrey Wolcott, GKW Working Design and Gristmill Builders

pp. 104, 168: lighting fixture and sink, Eleek

p. 106: designer, Joanne Palmisano

pp. 109, 120: designer, The Cushman Design Group and Gristmill Builders

pp. 127, 221: Sweeney Design Build

p. 133: designers, Joanne Palmisano and Nate Carr; fireplace builder, Church Hill Landscapes, Inc.

p. 140: designer, Roger Riley

p. 141: architect, John McLeod; builder, Northern Timbers Construction

p. 144: Silver Maple Construction

pp. 171, 173, 174, 215: Conant Metal & Light, Burlington, Vermont

pp. 172, 250: architect, Selin + Selin Architecture; builder, Peregrine Design Build

pp. 216, 226, 235: architect, Nathan Good Architects

p. 217: Mitra Design Studio

p. 219: architect, Brian Mac, Birdseye Architecture & Building; builder, Gristmill Builders

p. 229: Cowey de Vasselot Architects